"In today's world of 'whatever,' making good choices is becoming an increasingly difficult task. Kendra Smiley has tackled this very important issue with her trademark wisdom and humor."

WAYNE RICE
Director, Understanding Your Teenager Seminars
Co-founder, Youth Specialties

"Kendra Smiley's approach to teaching children how to make godly decisions offers real hope to nervous parents. Her down-to-earth style and "real mom" experience remind parents that we really can help our kids make good decisions."

CARLA BARNHILL
Editor, *Christian Parenting Today*

"We cannot make our children's choices for them, but we can provide a solid foundation from which their choices will be made. If we do this well, our children will become salt and light in a tasteless and dark world."

DON W. OTIS
Author, *Teach Your Children Well* and
Trickle-Down Morality

Helping Your Kids
Make Good Choices

Guiding Your Kids in a World Full of Options

Encouraging Parents of All Ages and Stages

KENDRA SMILEY

SERVANT PUBLICATIONS
ANN ARBOR, MICHIGAN

Vine Books is an imprint of Servant Publications especially designed to serve
evangelical Christians.

Published by Servant Publications
P.O. Box 8617
Ann Arbor, Michigan 48107

Cover design: Alan Furst, Minneapolis, Minnesota

00 01 02 03 10 9 8 7 6 5 4 3 2

Printed in the United States of America
ISBN 1-56955-157-X

LIBRARY OF CONGRESS CATALOGING-IN-PUBLICATION DATA

Smiley, Kendra, 1952–
Helping your kids make good choices : guiding your kids in a world full of
options, encouraging parents of all ages and stages / by Kendra Smiley.
     p.   cm.
Includes bibliographical references.
ISBN 1-56955-157-X (alk. paper)
1. Child rearing.   2. Child rearing—Religious aspects—Christianity.
3. Decision making.   I. Title

HQ769.3 .S65 2000
248.8'45—dc21   00-032080

Dedication

*To kids of all ages who desire
to make good choices.*

Contents

Foreword

This book is about you, as a parent, helping your kids make good choices. To be honest, we have no experience in being parents, but we do know what it is like to be kids. Our parents, John and Kendra Smiley, have encouraged good choices throughout our lives.

Mom has written this book using biblical principles and life experiences to show the ways in which parents can help their kids make good choices. The people who know us can tell you that the three of us do not always make perfect choices. This book, even if read four or five times, cannot ensure that your kids will make *every* right decision. It does, however, present a wonderful guideline you can follow to give your kids the best chance possible to make the right choices. Through modeling, encouraging, and guiding your children to make good choices, you will be confident, when the time comes, to allow them to make decisions on their own.

No parents are perfect, as any kid will tell you, but we three are thankful for the fact that our parents took the time and energy to find the best way to help their kids make the right choices. We hope you enjoy this book, and remember, no matter how old your kids are or what walk of life you are in, you can always strive to help your kids make good choices.

Matthew, Aaron, and Jonathan Smiley

Acknowledgments

Writing a book can be a very isolated, somewhat lonely experience. It is not, however, done in isolation or all alone. There are many people who have contributed to this book but do not have their names on the cover.

First and foremost, I want to thank my husband, John, by far the best parent (and husband) I personally know. He has modeled, encouraged, and guided each thought and concept in this book. And he has allowed me the opportunity to "slack off" in some areas of responsibility to accept the opportunity and responsibility of writing.

It would seem that you can't write a book about "Helping Your Kids Make Good Choices" without having the blessing of kids. Our sons, Matthew, Aaron, and Jonathan, are my guinea pigs, my delight, and my examples of young men who, more often than not, make good choices. Thank you, gentlemen, for writing the foreword to this book and for making the difficult task of parenting such a joy (especially in retrospect)!

Thanks to Pam, my sounding board, my dear friend, my confidante, and the balancer of my calendar. You are a gift from God! Thank you to Kathy Deering of Servant Publications who was not only my editor, but a prayer warrior throughout this project.

And most importantly, thanks to Jesus—"the author and perfecter of our faith" (Hebrews 12:2).

Introduction

It was a beautiful fall day—just cool enough to remind you that summer had passed and just warm and sunny enough to make you forget that winter's blast would soon arrive. The high school bell rang two hours before its usual time. Classes were being dismissed early today for the annual homecoming parade. Floats and convertibles were maneuvering to their appointed positions in the procession. Marching band members, decked out in their stately red and white uniforms, filled in their ranks at the head of the parade. The cheerleaders climbed onto the fire truck with the varsity football players, and finishing touches were being made to the hometown cavalcade. Students who were not in the parade were beginning to line the parade route, preparing to cheer for their classmates and enjoy the break from the rigors of the classroom.

Well, *most* of the students lined the route. Watching the parade was not mandatory. No one was taking attendance. But if it had been taken, Jodi, Sheila, and Kim would have been marked absent. The parade might be fun, but they had another idea of how they would have fun today. Sheila's mom and dad were both at work and the girls headed for her house. Once inside, they went straight to the liquor cabinet.

"Won't your parents be mad?" asked Kim.

"They'll never notice," Sheila replied. "They don't keep track of how much stuff they have in here. We'll just sample some from lots of different bottles instead of drinking from only one."

"Sounds like a plan to me," said Jodi as she grabbed a glass. "What have you got?"

"Try this," Sheila offered as she poured some foul-smelling brown liquid into Jodi's glass.

After a quick sniff, Jodi drank a big gulp. "Gosh, that was awful!" she sputtered. "Let me try something else."

Before long, each of the girls had consumed the equivalent of two or three stiff drinks. Jodi had definitely downed more than anyone else.

"I'm not feeling good," she finally moaned, holding her stomach. "I think I'm going to be sick."

"Get her outside," Sheila commanded. "My mom will be really mad if someone throws up on her living room carpet!"

The girls moved as fast as they could, pushing Jodi through the dining room, the kitchen, and finally out the back door. By that time Jodi was retching. They barely got to the yard before she began to throw up. She vomited for about five minutes and then without warning, she passed out.

"Do you think she's OK?" Kim asked.

"I don't know. She had a lot to drink," Sheila replied.

"We've got to do something!" said Kim, getting more excited by the moment. "She might die! She might be dead now!! Does she have a pulse?"

"I'll check her," Sheila said, trying to appear calm. "You go inside and call her mom."

"Not me. Her parents are going to be furious. You call them."

"Well, *someone* has to call! This is serious!!"

The Phone Call

Would you want to receive that phone call? Do you want to answer the phone and hear that your fourteen-year-old daughter has passed out from drinking?

How about the phone call that informs you that your ten-year-old has been picked up for shoplifting and is being held by the authorities?

Or the call from the junior high school office telling you that your twelve-year-old (the one you dropped off at school one hour before) is not in attendance?

Do you want to receive any of these calls or any ones like them? Of course not! Every parent hopes that their child will make better choices than the ones Jodi, Kim, and Sheila made. Or the ones made by the shoplifting ten-year-old. Or the twelve-year-old truant.

As parents we want our children to make good choices, ones that will result in a healthy, happy, godly lifestyle. We *want* that, but is *wanting* it enough?

The obvious answer is "No." There is a major difference between *wanting* something to happen and making the effort to see that it happens. *Wanting* to lose ten pounds is different from actually losing ten pounds. Losing weight takes effort and commitment. It demands certain disciplines and behaviors. And it is that behavior, discipline, commitment, and effort that produces results. *Wanting* (or wishing or hoping) hardly ever produces results. "The sluggard craves and gets nothing, but the desires of the diligent are fully satisfied" (Proverbs 13:4).

So what effort, commitment, discipline, and behavior are necessary to help our kids make good choices? I'm glad you asked. The pages of this book are dedicated to answering that very question. We'll divide our pursuit of the answer into two sections. The first section will deal with the actual process of making good choices. This will serve as the foundation for our study. In order to help our kids make good choices, we must first understand how *anyone*—ourselves included—can make good choices.

Then we will deal specifically with the role of parents and the influence a parent has over the decision-making process that children employ. Because there are different stages of parenting, this section will examine three sets of parents. Lisa and Brian are both Christians (see appendix) and they are expecting their first child. Their situation is different from Joan and Andy's. Joan and Andy recently accepted Christ (see appendix) and began to attend church. Their children, two sons, are still at home, but both of them have already reached double digits. Ruth and James, our third couple, have one child who is no longer living under their roof and one child still at home.

Each age and stage of parenting is different. Although we can all see the beauty in starting early to help our kids make good choices (like Lisa and Brian), there are things we can do at every stage.

In the examination of these parenting stages, we will look at the MEGA guidelines (Modeling, Encouraging, Guiding, and Allowing) and we will take a specific look at some of the "biggies" when it comes to the choices our kids will make—sex, drugs, and Jesus. The decisions our children make about these important issues are a part of the tip of an iceberg. With an iceberg, the part that shows above the water is only about 10 percent of the entire mass. Below the water level is the majority of the iceberg. The choices our children make about sex, drugs, and Jesus are choices that show. The foundation that we have laid for our children, hopefully before they make those decisions, is 90 percent of the mass below. The basic decision-making process and the specific guidelines that we follow (the MEGA guidelines) can create a solid foundation for the decisions our kids will make.

This firm foundation can help our kids make good choices. Without the proper base of support, it is *difficult* for the tip of the iceberg to illustrate good choices. It is *not*, however, impossible. Also, there is no guarantee that a solid foundation, an understanding of the decision-making process, and a sincere effort to apply the MEGA guidelines of parenting will unequivocally produce positive choices. Remember, we're examining how to "help" our kids make good choices. The title of this book is *not* how to make good choices for your kids or how to force your kids to make good choices. It is *Helping Your Kids Make Good Choices.* Our goal is to positively influence the choices our children will make.

Even in light of the above disclaimer, the odds of good choices at the tip of the iceberg are significantly increased if the foundation is carefully and prayerfully created. That is all part of the effort, commitment, discipline, and behavior that we will examine.

But first, a reminder of how important and how prolific choices are....

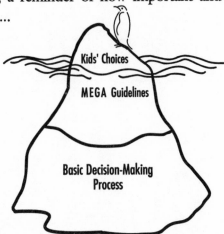

Kids' Choices

MEGA Guidelines

Basic Decision-Making Process

We All Make Choices— It's Inevitable!

Then choose for yourselves this day whom you will serve, whether the gods your forefathers served beyond the River, or the gods of the Amorites, in whose land you are living. But as for me and my household, we will serve the Lord.

JOSHUA 24:15b

Life is filled with choices. Why, just today you chose when you would get up and what you would put on. You chose what you would eat for breakfast (if you chose to eat breakfast at all). You chose to pick up this book and you are now choosing to read it.

"No, wait just a minute," you protest. "Those haven't all been my choices. I *have to* get up at 6:00 A.M. I have no choice. If I don't get up at 6:00 A.M., I can't get a load of wash done before everyone starts their showers."

But it is your choice to wash in the morning and not in the evening. You made that choice which leads (quite logically) to your choice to rise and shine at 6:00 A.M.

"Well, maybe you're right about that one, but I have to wear a uniform to work. No choices there!"

What about your choice to work at that particular location or in that particular occupation? That choice was yours.

"True, true. But you're wrong about the next one. My

doctor has me on a pretty strict diet. He makes my breakfast choices." (Gotcha!)

Good point, but it is your choice (and a wise one) to follow your doctor's orders. Many years ago your parents might have been able to force you to eat this or that, but as adults, the choice is ours.

For a small portion of our children's lives, we are in complete control and we make all the choices for them. Then we begin to allow them the responsibility of making choices and our role is to help them make good choices. Ultimately our children are adults and the choices are theirs alone.

> Do you want pigtails or ponytails?
> Do you want to sit on Mommy's lap or Daddy's lap?
> Do you want to play a game or watch a video?
> Do you want milk or juice?
> Do you want the socks with ruffles or the plain ones?
> Do you want the red crayon or the green one?

The choices begin at an early age and continue. When our children go to school they have even more choices to make and typically we are not there for guidance.

> Do you want chocolate milk or white milk?
> Do you want sack lunch or hot lunch?
> Do you want to play four-square or kick ball?
> Do you want to study spelling or stare out the window?
> Do you want to get your work done or miss recess?
> Do you want one scoop or two?

And it doesn't end in the early grades. As freedom and inter-personal relationships expand, so do the choices.

Do you want to tease the
new girl or make friends with her?
Do you want to copy Jim's test paper or do your own work?
Do you want to go out for the basketball team or not?
Do you want to tell Shannon's best friend to tell Shannon to
tell Jane to tell Sally to tell Rachel that Bill told Sam who told
Mike that Chris wants to "go out" with her, or not?

Junior and senior high school students have no fewer choices, only choices with more dramatic consequences.

Do you want to drink or stay sober?
Do you want to date this person
or that person or no person?
Do you want to study or not?
Do you want to remain a virgin or lose your virginity?

Actually, let's go back and edit *all* of those questions. Rather than asking "Do you *want* …," let's substitute the words "Do you *choose* …" Part of our responsibility as parents is to teach our children that life is filled with choices and the best choice is not necessarily what they *want*. A good choice is not automatically synonymous with choosing what we *want*. That realization is one aspect of choosing wisely.

Choices are made each day in regard to every part of our lives including our health, our intellect, our character, and our relationships with God and others. Since choices are so numerous and varied, we need to begin to build the foundation for helping our kids make good choices by taking a look at the basic concept of choosing wisely.

ONE

Choosing Wisely

A wise son brings joy to his father.

PROVERBS 10:1a

Making a good choice, a wise choice, is often synonymous with making a godly choice. I heard a speaker declare once that wisdom is seeing things from God's point of view. The wise choice does not have to make you happy or be what you want in order to be a good choice. More importantly it must be in sync with God's Word. A choice is not a good one if it contradicts the Word of God. "Keeping God's commands is what counts" (1 Corinthians 7:19b).

If any of you lacks wisdom, he should ask God, who gives generously to all without finding fault, and it will be given to him.

JAMES 1:5

This passage lets you know without a doubt that we as human beings are capable of choosing wisely. In fact, I am certain that each of you could make a list of various wise choices you have made through the years.

Perhaps that list would include your choice of a spouse or your choice in career selection. Did you include on it your choice of a home or neighborhood? Did you put down your choice to have children? The list could be very long.

When you make a wise choice, it is probable that you consciously or unconsciously employ three simple keys. When it's time to make a decision, the first thing most people do is to weigh the pros and cons. In making good choices, we are so accustomed to doing this mental evaluation that we usually do it unconsciously.

For example, on a very elementary level, I drive up to the fast food restaurant and glance through the list of options on the drive-up menu. My biggest choice is burger versus grilled chicken. As I evaluate the choice, I unconsciously weigh the pros and cons of each entrée.

Grilled Chicken: + good taste
                       + fewer fat grams
Hamburger: + good taste
                 − more fat grams
                 − beef planned for dinner

Grilled chicken wins the contest! The choice was made rapidly.

At other times a choice is more complicated, or isn't as common and familiar. At these junctures, we are more aware of the process of choosing and occasionally more baffled by the choice we must make.

I remember many years ago when I had to do some very serious weighing of pros and cons. Before my children were born, I was an elementary school teacher. I began my first teaching job in the state of Illinois five weeks into the school year. The fourth-grade teacher's husband was transferred and I was hired to take her position. I thoroughly enjoyed my year and my students and began friendships with other faculty members that continue to this day.

In April of that school year, however, the school board made an announcement that directly affected me. Because of a shortage of funding, they stated their intention to cut programs and release several teachers. There would be a reorganization of responsibility and the teachers most recently hired would be the first to go.

There was no question who was the newest teacher. I didn't even start on the first day of school. *Everyone* (including my fourth-graders) had seniority on me.

As this dilemma unfolded, many teachers began to look for positions in other schools. So did I. I was offered a sixth-grade teaching job in a nearby town and almost simultaneously was offered the eighth-grade language arts position at the school where I was currently teaching.

What choice should I make? It was definitely time to weigh the pros and cons. I divided a piece of paper into two columns and headed each column with the name of one of the schools. Then I began the process.

Old School:	**New School:**
+ familiar	− unfamiliar
+ excellent principal	− unknown administration
+ friends on the staff	− no acquaintances on staff
− teaching an unfamiliar subject	+ teaching familiar subjects
− no experience with new grade level	+ grade level I enjoyed
− district financially unstable	+ district financially stable
	+ salary increase
	+ more coaching opportunities

When the list was finished, I realized that the new school was the winner. Just like the grilled chicken sandwich, the pros outweighed the cons.

Pro Versus Con

A young man I had known for years contacted me one day and asked if we could talk. Since I have been in senior-high youth ministry for years, this was not unusual. We arranged to get together on a Sunday afternoon. I knew this young man, Ned, had been struggling with college and career, but I had no idea about the particulars of his situation. As we walked and talked, he filled me in.

"Kendra," he began, "I've really managed to get myself into a mess. I am deeply in debt to a whole lot of people." He then began to list how he had borrowed money from his parents, his friends, and even people at work. He said he had college loans and credit card bills and didn't see any way out. "I've been on a spending spree for the last four years and I've dug a pretty deep pit," he said.

So this was the circumstance that was haunting Ned. Even though I am not a financial planning professional, I knew that I might be able to help him examine some of the good choices which had the potential to expedite his climb out of the pit of debt he had created.

"Ned, this is quite a mess, but you've definitely taken the first step by admitting the problem and wanting to do something about it," I said. Then I suggested that we list the ways Ned was spending money to brainstorm how he could slowly work his way out of the problem.

We went through some of his expenditures and thought of ways to eliminate them or at least to decrease them. For instance, Ned lived alone in an apartment.

"Have you ever thought about moving back home with your parents for awhile?" I asked. "I don't know if they'd be amenable to that suggestion, but it would save you quite a bit of money."

Ned said they wouldn't mind. "And I doubt if they would even charge me anything for room and board."

We seemed to have hit on an idea that had some potential. We decided to look at the pros and cons.

Own Apartment:	**Parents' Home:**
+ freedom	− less freedom
+ pets	− no animals
− rent bill	+ free rent
− food bill	+ free food
− utility bill	+ free utilities
	+ enjoy parents' company
	+ able to help them

The pros of the possible move were overwhelmingly greater. It was an idea worth contemplating further.

For adults and kids alike, weighing the pros and cons is one key to making wise choices. "She considers a field and buys it" (Proverbs 31:16a). "Considering" whether or not to buy the field would likely include weighing the pros and cons. Or how about this example from the Bible.

"The Lord said to Moses, 'Send some men to explore the land of Canaan, which I am giving to the Israelites. From each ancestral tribe send one of its leaders.'" So Moses did what God commanded and sent out twelve men to explore the land. After forty days they returned, and gave Moses this account: "We went into the land to which you sent us, and it does flow with milk and honey! Here is its fruit. But the people who live there are powerful, and the cities are fortified and very large" (Numbers 13:1-2, 27-28a).

Milk and honey: a pro. Powerful people, fortified and large cities: three big cons.

Hmmm. It seemed that the cons outweighed the pros. But wait! All the facts had not been evaluated. It is very important to consider *every* possible aspect.

> Joshua son of Nun and Caleb son of Jophunneh, who were among those who had explored the land, tore their clothes and said to the entire Israelite assembly, "The land we passed through and explored is exceedingly good. If the Lord is pleased with us, he will lead us into that land, a land flowing with milk and honey, and will give it to us. Only do not rebel against the Lord. And do not be afraid of the people of the land, because we will swallow them up. Their protection is gone, but the Lord is with us. Do not be afraid of them."
>
> NUMBERS 14:6-9

Let's take another look at the pros and cons.

The Pros:	**The Cons:**
+ good land	− powerful people
+ land flowing with milk and honey	− fortified cities
+ enemies' protection gone	− large cities
+++ God's promise of the land	

Upon closer examination, the pros far outweighed the cons. The pluses were greater than the minuses. The minority report of Joshua and Caleb remembered to factor in a very important aspect ignored by the other ten men. Joshua and Caleb recalled the promise of God. "Send some men to explore the land of Canaan which *I am giving* to the Israelites" (Numbers 13:1, my emphasis). Oops! Ten spies had forgotten that promise. God's promise—his plan—was a big positive element. Way too big to ignore.

Unfortunately, God's promise *was* ignored and the majority report was accepted. As a result, the Israelites wandered in the wilderness for a whole generation! This is one case where it would have really paid off to weigh *all* the pros and cons. That is a good thing to remember.

Seeking Wise Counsel

In addition to weighing the pros and cons, a wise choice is enhanced by seeking counsel.

"The way of a fool seems right to him, but a wise man listens to advice" (Proverbs 12:15).

"Listen to advice and accept instruction, and in the end you will be wise" (Proverbs 19:20).

"Make plans by seeking advice ..." (Proverbs 20:18a).

Just any old counsel won't do, however, if our desire is to make a good choice. God's Word is very clear about the importance of seeking *wise* counsel.

Blessed is the man who does not walk in the counsel of the wicked or stand in the way of sinners or sit in the seat of mockers. But his delight is in the law of the Lord, and on his law he meditates day and night. He is like a tree planted by streams of water, which yields its fruit in season and whose leaf does not wither. Whatever he does prospers.

PSALM 1:1-3

We are not to seek counsel from the wicked. We are instead to find *wise* counsel. When I decided it was time to make a wise choice in regard to the teaching position options so many years ago, I employed this second key in addition to weighing the pros and cons. Remember that I put together a list of pluses and minuses? I did so with the help of my principal. He was an outstanding educator, had experience in many of the county schools and, even more importantly, he was a committed Christian. Bill was definitely able to provide wise counsel.

Ned, the young man attempting to dig out of the pit of debt he had created, was looking for counsel on that Sunday afternoon walk. He chose to ask an adult he knew had his best interests at heart and who, in his experience, had tried to encourage people to live by the principles in God's Word.

Can you name a person or a ministry that has made choices with the aid of unwise counsel? Someone who chose "agreeing" counsel rather than wise counsel? It is an age old story.

Rehoboam went to Shechem, for all the Israelites had gone there to make him king. When Jeroboam son of Nebat heard this (he was still in Egypt, where he had fled from King Solomon), he returned from Egypt. So they sent for Jeroboam, and he and the whole assembly of Israel went to Rehoboam and said to him: "Your father put a heavy yoke on us, but now lighten the harsh labor and the heavy yoke he put on us, and we will serve you."

Rehoboam answered, "Go away for three days and then come back to me." So the people went away.

Then King Rehoboam consulted the elders who had served his father Solomon during his lifetime. "How would you advise me to answer these people?" he asked.

They replied, "If today you will be a servant to these people and serve them and give them a favorable answer, they will always be your servants."

But Rehoboam rejected the advice the elders gave him and consulted the young men who had grown up with him and were serving him. He asked them, "What is your advice? How should we answer these people who say to me, 'Lighten the yoke your father put on us'?"

The young men who had grown up with him replied, "Tell these people who have said to you, 'Your father put a heavy yoke on us, but make our yoke lighter'—tell them, 'My little finger is thicker than my father's waist. My father laid on you a heavy yoke; I will make it even heavier. My father scourged you with whips; I will scourge you with scorpions....'"

When all Israel saw that the king refused to listen to them, they answered the king: "What share do we have in David, what part in Jesse's son? To your tents, O Israel! Look after your own house, O David!" So the Israelites went home.

1 KINGS 12:1-11,16

The king lost his servants. If he had followed the advice of the elders, things would have probably gone much differently. Instead he listened to the advisors who told him what he *wanted* to hear. (There's that word *want* again.) In order to choose wisely, to make good choices, we must utilize wise counsel.

Evict the Emotion

These two keys—weighing the pros and cons, and seeking wise counsel—are not necessarily enough. Even when utilizing both of them we can still make a poor choice. A third key is important: we must evict the emotion in our decision making. Consider the rich young ruler.

"Now a man came up to Jesus and asked, 'Teacher, what good thing must I do to get eternal life?'" (Matthew 19:16) This man was seeking wise counsel.

"'Why do you ask me about what is good?' Jesus replied. 'There is only One who is good. If you want to enter life, obey the commandments.'

"'Which ones?' the man inquired.

Jesus' reply: "'Do not murder, do not commit adultery, do not steal, do not give false testimony, honor your father and mother, and love your neighbor as yourself'" (vv. 17-18).

The rich young ruler weighed these words. He discovered that in his personal evaluation, his pros far outweighed his cons.

"'All these I have kept,' the young man said. 'What do I still lack?'" (v. 20)

Jesus replied with a statement that evoked great emotion in the heart of the rich young man. "If you want to be perfect, go, sell your possessions and give to the poor, and you will have treasure in heaven. Then come, follow me" (v. 21).

"When the young man heard this, he went away sad, because he had great wealth" (v. 22). The young man was sad. He didn't *want* to sell his possessions and give to the poor. He loved his things more than he desired eternal life. His love of possessions ruled his decision-making ability and he was sad. His heart ruled his intellect and he did not choose to follow Jesus. Instead he made a poor choice, with eternal consequences.

The rich young ruler sought counsel—the wisest counsel available. He had pondered the pros and cons of the words of Jesus. But ultimately he came up short. Perhaps it was because of his lack of understanding of the eternal risk involved in not choosing Christ. Not choosing Jesus is the greatest "con" possible. Or perhaps his problem was not setting aside the emotion. Emotions can be powerful and persuasive.

Remember the story of Christ walking on the water?

> During the fourth watch of the night Jesus went out to them, walking on the lake. When the disciples saw him walking on the lake, they were terrified. "It's a ghost," they said, and cried out in fear.
>
> But Jesus immediately said to them: "Take courage! It is I. Don't be afraid."
>
> "Lord, if it's you," Peter replied, "tell me to come to you on the water."
>
> "Come," he said.
>
> Then Peter got down out of the boat and walked on the water to Jesus.
>
> MATTHEW 14:25-29

Peter initially managed to ignore his emotion of fear and he walked out to Jesus on the water. Unfortunately the fear returned and his feelings took over. Then he was no longer "on top of things." "But when he saw the wind, he was afraid and, beginning to sink, cried out, 'Lord, save me!'" (v. 30).

His choice to let his emotion (fear, in this case) rule almost cost him his life. Emotions are powerful things that can alter our ability to make wise choices. That is why tossing out the emotion, giving it no place in the wise decision-making process, is another key in that process.

Please understand. Emotion is a wonderful part of being alive. Nothing is more moving than an emotionally charged sermon or the passion-filled words of a child or spouse. But emotions can be like blinders, narrowing our vision and perspective.

God knows this, of course. For instance, he warned us about letting one emotion—worry—influence our choices, and instructed us in Matthew 6:25-27 not to let the emotion of worry have power over us.

> "Therefore I tell you, do not worry about your life, what you will eat or drink; or about your body, what you will wear. Is not life more important than food, and the body more important than clothes? Look at the birds of the air; they do not sow or reap or store away in barns, and yet your heavenly Father feeds them. Are you not much more valuable than they? Who of you by worrying can add a single hour to his life?"

God knew that worry could distract us and keep us from making good choices. Instead his instruction is to "Seek first his kingdom and his righteousness, and all these things will be given to you as well" (v. 33). We need to evict the emotion to make a good choice.

As a fourth-grade teacher with an important choice to make, I sat across from the principal's desk and together we weighed the pros and cons. He provided wise counsel on the decision I had to make regarding my teaching position.

"But Bill," I finally added as I realized the wise choice seemed to be a change in schools, "I'll really miss this teaching staff. And the kids have been so great. I'll miss them. I'm not sure I *want* to move to another school district."

What was I saying? My emotions were calling me to stay. I didn't want to face a change or leave the pluses of my current job. Was that, however, a wise choice?

No. It was a feeling. It was not the basis for a good choice. Instead, it was a reflection of my emotions. In order to make a good choice, I realized that I would have to evict the emotion— throw it out and then examine the facts.

The truth of the matter was that the teaching staff I admired was no longer going to be intact. Many of them were finding teaching positions elsewhere. And the kids I loved? They were all moving to the next grade level. Undoubtedly, there would be great staff and extra special students at the new school too. I had to evict the emotion for a good choice.

And how about Ned, the young man with money problems? As we moved down the list of pros and cons about a possible move back to his parents' home, one aspect brought forth a great deal of emotion from him. A con to his moving was not being able to keep his dogs.

"Kendra, if I move home," he told me, "I'll have to do something with my dogs because Mom and Dad won't want them in their house. I don't want to have to find other homes for them."

Although I am definitely not an animal person, I do have one son who is, so I tried to imagine that son and his love for animals as I gently answered.

"Sometimes, as adults, we have to make tough decisions," I told Ned. Even though he was very fond of his dogs, it was important to evaluate his thinking after removing that emotion. "I'm sure you could find good homes for them if that is the choice you make," I told him. "You have to decide what is ultimately the better choice for your situation. It is up to you."

Setting aside emotion is crucial in making a good choice. That doesn't make the decision a cold-hearted one, it merely makes it a more intellectual one.

One of the most vivid examples of the effectiveness of this key principal can be illustrated by a recommendation we have shared with our youth-group teenagers through the years.

For over sixteen years, my husband John and I have been volunteer youth leaders at our church. There are certain lessons and topics we have been sure to rotate through our program so that each class has heard them at least one time. One such message is our presentation on the Bible and sex. (This one is always well attended, as you can imagine. Our own teenagers, however, have been caught cringing at the thought of their parents talking about and teaching about sex in youth group.) In the lesson, we present biblical principles and bring into focus the truth from God's Word. We also discuss the fact that there are some gray areas.

For example, courting (as opposed to dating) has become an accepted and encouraged practice in many Christian persuasions. Does God condemn what we traditionally call dating? Not that I can see. Does he demand it? Certainly not. This is an example of a gray area.

Behavior in dating has gray areas also and some definite black-and-white ones. Fornication (the avoidance of it) is a black-and-white issue in the Bible. A kiss is not addressed—a gray area. (We're not talking about Romans 16:16, greeting "one another with a holy kiss.") So we tell the kids that they will have to determine where they will draw their "line in the sand."

After we give them this information and challenge, we make a very significant suggestion.

"Because you have to make some personal decisions in this arena, I would encourage you to do so very soon. In fact, next Saturday morning while you are eating your cereal, decide where you will draw your line in the sand. What will you consider appropriate and inappropriate on a date?"

Why do I suggest they make that decision on Saturday morning while they eat their cereal? Because the average teenager has very little emotion to evict at that time on a Saturday. Their eyes are still matted shut. Their mouths are only open wide enough to slip the spoon in. And, most likely, their elbows are on the table with their chin resting gently in a cupped palm. No emotions there! (Unless a coma-like state has emotions.) It's a perfect time to consider an issue which could be packed with emotion by that evening.

At ten o'clock on Saturday night, the average teen is likely to be experiencing much more emotion and may have input contrary to the information presented at youth group or more importantly the wisdom of God's Word.

So we tell them to draw their line in the sand in the morning while eating their cereal. What are we really saying? Set aside the emotion and you'll make a wiser choice.

As Gayle Roper put it so well in her book, *Balancing Your Emotions,* "Emotions leave us at the mercy of others and ourselves."[1]

Our best hope for making good choices—wise and godly choices—is to employ all three keys. To (1) weigh the pros and cons; (2) seek wise counsel; and (3) evict the emotion. When we do all three of these things we are more likely to choose wisely. And practicing the art of making good choices is at the very base of our foundation.

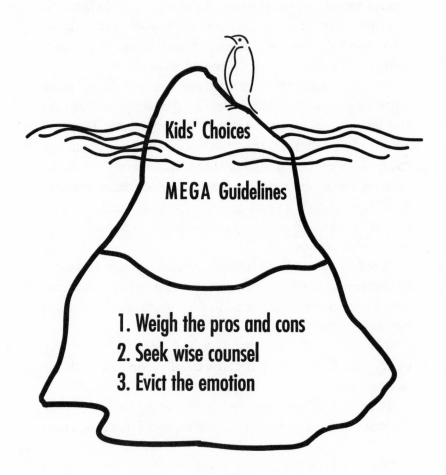

Kids' Choices

MEGA Guidelines

1. Weigh the pros and cons
2. Seek wise counsel
3. Evict the emotion

TWO

Choosing Foolishly

But a foolish son [brings] grief to his mother.

PROVERBS 10:1b

As we continue to evaluate the art of making choices as the foundation for helping your kids make good choices, we are compelled to take a look at bad choices. If choosing wisely or making a good choice is in sync with making a godly choice, then choosing foolishly many times means choosing contrary to the wisdom of God.

> Therefore everyone who hears these words of mine and puts them into practice is like a wise man who built his house on the rock. The rain came down, the streams rose, and the winds blew and beat against that house; yet it did not fall, because it had its foundation on the rock. But everyone who hears these words of mine and does not put them into practice is like a foolish man who built his house on sand. The rain came down, the streams rose, and the winds blew and beat against that house, and it fell with a great crash.
>
> MATTHEW 7:24-27

A wise person is one who hears *and* puts into practice the Word of God. That is a good choice. A fool is one who hears the Word and does *not* act on it—a bad choice.

I *would* ask if any of you have ever made any bad choices, but since I already know the answer, I don't want to tempt anyone to lie. Just as I am sure that each of you has made wise choices, it is safe to assume that you have also made some foolish or unwise choices. Eliminating bad choices is impossible, but it *is* possible to reduce the number and frequency of bad choices and to refrain from repeating the *same* ones over and over again.

I can still vividly recall foolish decisions I made as a child. Like the time I disobeyed my mother's instruction not to go to Eric's house with a group of my friends. She said that I was not allowed to go, but I, being an impudent thirteen-year-old, knew it was fine if I went *and* that she would never find out anyway. Wrong on both counts! When I was pushed into Eric's swimming pool by one of my friends, the jig was up! There was no way to dry off and make it home on time. Mom discovered my disobedience and it was *not* fine after all. My choice was a bad one.

Unfortunately, it was not my only bad choice. I had made others prior to the forbidden swim in Eric's pool, and I continued to make them after I dried off. The "D" I got on my final exam in Algebra 1 as a high school freshman was actually the culmination of several bad choices. (Thank goodness the exam was only a small percentage of the final grade!) As a child, I not only made the occasional bad choice about classroom work, but I also made some bad choices when it came to how I treated others. More than once I made a bad choice about where to go and with whom and I even made bad choices about alerting (actually *not* alerting) my parents to many of my choices. (I think I'd better stop now. My mom, now in her 80s, reads my books and I don't have time to suffer my discipline in retrospect.)

Sometimes my poor choices brought immediate discipline or consequences, but occasionally it seemed as though I had miraculously escaped any disclosure or repercussions. Actually, we mistakenly presume that if we are not "caught" in our bad choice then we have "gotten away with it." The major fallacy in that thinking is to assume that God has taken time off and is momentarily not omnipresent. It doesn't happen.

As volunteer high school youth leaders we have had many opportunities to see both the good and bad choices kids make. I remember a time when we took our group to play miniature golf. After everyone had finished the eighteen holes, we handed in our clubs, paid our bill, and headed for the parking lot. About ten feet from one of the vans, a young man in our group stopped me.

"Look what I've got," he said with a rather arrogant tone. And then he showed me a golf ball that he had stolen from the course. "I picked this up and carried it out and nobody saw me," he continued with as much boldness as he could muster.

The whole exchange was very interesting to me. He knew beyond a shadow of a doubt that I did not approve of what he had done or find it the least bit amusing. *I* knew that if he had really wanted to keep the ball, he would not have shown it to me.

So why were we standing in the parking lot of the miniature golf course staring at a golf ball with an identifying orange stripe around its middle? I believe that this young man showed the ball to me as a test. What would I say? What would I do? Would I make him return the ball? Would I be too embarrassed?

His words were just out of his mouth when I began to chuckle. The teen could see nothing particularly funny and looked at me with disbelief.

"You think nobody saw you?" I asked, still chuckling. "Do

you think God had his eyes closed? Do you think you *got away* with something? For a fifty-cent golf ball, you've chosen to break one of God's Ten Commandments. Is that a good choice?"

That was it. I didn't reprimand him or give him any instructions. I just turned and headed for the van. This young man already knew he had not made a good choice. He did not need for me to point that out. He needed a reminder of God's omnipresence. He paused and then walked back to the miniature golf park where he returned the ball to the attendant. Evidently he realized the error of his ways.

He had made two mistakes. The first was stealing someone else's property (a foolish choice) and the second one was imagining that his unwise choice had gone undetected. There is no such thing as "getting away with it." There are always consequences—even if they are not immediate.

> The Lord is slow to anger, abounding in love and forgiving sin and rebellion. Yet he does not leave the guilty unpunished.
>
> NUMBERS 14:18a

Wayne Rice, co-founder of the Youth Specialties ministry, speaks in his "Understanding Your Teenager" curriculum of two types of consequences: natural and logical. Natural consequences are those that follow naturally. If a child touches a hot stove, he gets burned. The burn is a natural consequence of touching something hot.

The school child who does not take his lunch money will not be able to buy lunch—a natural consequence.

The young man who steals a golf ball from the miniature golf course will not be trusted 100 percent by his youth leader—a natural consequence.

The natural consequences of some poor choices have more impact than others. Some are more severe. And some are more visible. The unmarried teenage girl who becomes pregnant and chooses to give birth to her baby carries a very visible sign of her poor choice to have sex before marriage. The unmarried teenage girl who becomes pregnant and chooses to abort her child still has consequences for her poor choice, they are just less visible to the average passerby.

Every teenage girl experimenting with sex runs the risk of becoming pregnant. That is a natural consequence. Every teenage boy or girl experimenting with sex runs the risk of other physical and psychological consequences even if pregnancy is avoided or terminated. These are also natural consequences of the foolish choice.

Natural consequences follow naturally. No one has to enforce them. They are almost involuntary. Logical consequences on the other hand, are typically assigned and agreed upon in advance of the transgression or poor choice.

We tell a five-year-old to stay in the yard or he will have to come inside. If he chooses to defy the instructions given to him and he leaves the yard, the logical consequence is put into effect and he comes inside.

A rule is established regarding curfew—for every fifteen minutes after the designated deadline, the offender will be expected to be in one hour earlier the next time. That is an example of a logical consequence. A teen who chooses to be in one hour late might as well cancel the next outing because the logical consequences would indicate that his curfew time would be four hours earlier!

All choices have consequences—natural, logical, or otherwise. Foolish choices typically have negative consequences.

Now, before (1) the inevitability of making bad choices and (2) the reality of each bad choice having a negative consequence overwhelm you, let me suggest that foolish choices are not totally useless. Bad choices can be a source of experience which can lead to life lessons.

In *Give Your Heart a Good Spring Cleaning* I introduced readers to the patient and practically perfect parent with kind, compassionate, caring, cum laude kids (purely fictional) who was interviewed by the practicing, persistent parent. The intent of the interview was to discover Super Mom's secret to success.

"You are such a great mother," said the new mom. "All six of your children are upstanding citizens. They have all accepted Christ. They are all leaders in their churches and communities. My question is a simple one: Where did you learn to be such a great mom?"

"That, my dear, is an easy question to answer," the older woman replied. "The answer is as simple as two words: good choices."

The new mom seemed a little baffled and was not satisfied with that answer. "May I ask you a second question?" she inquired.

"Absolutely!"

"How did you make those good choices?"

"Elementary. The answer is one simple word: experience."

Still not completely satisfied with the answers she was receiving, the inexperienced mom tried one more time. "I see, and would you be able to tell me where you got all that experience?" she asked, hoping to finally get to the bottom of things.

"Absolutely," the seasoned mom replied. "Bad choices!"[2]

If bad choices are converted into experience, they have the opportunity to become life lessons. My mother had told me not to go to Eric's house. I disobeyed and suffered the conse-quences—a very early curfew (right after supper, in fact) for the next week. I didn't enjoy this restriction on my life. In junior high, seven days of restriction can feel like a lifetime! I gained experience, however, and this experience strongly influenced my future choices to obey my mother's rules about my where-abouts. Disobeying her wasn't worth the risk of jeopardizing my freedom. (And I really hadn't had much fun at Eric's any-way.)

Bad choices can produce experience. And experience can become a life lesson. Life lessons can, in turn, produce good choices. But remember, our goal is to reduce the number and frequency of bad choices and to come as close as possible to eradicating them entirely. We don't HAVE to have life lessons in order to make a good choice. (See the previous chapter on making wise choices.)

As parents we have a strong desire to help our kids make good choices (hence this book) and consequently a passion to help our kids avoid bad choices. One of our strategies to accom-plish this is to use our own life lessons or the life lessons of oth-ers to illustrate what to avoid.

Our eldest son got his driver's license in the fall after his six-teenth birthday. Being from a farm family, our children enter the drivers' education car on the first day of class with quite a few miles logged on the tractor. This legal experience which they have acquired for several years prior to their official drivers' education serves them well. They have witnessed difficult situa-tions where driving decisions have had to be made. They have learned to judge distances and the size of their vehicles and they are generally more confident and competent than their urban counterparts.

One driving experience for which they have very little previous practice, however, is driving on ice. A tractor is only seldom out on the ice.

That chasm in Matthew's driving expertise was obvious one winter day the next year when he slid on a patch of ice and the truck ended up in the ditch. There was some damage done to the vehicle, but much more importantly, no damage was done to Matthew. When he and his dad finally pulled the truck from the ditch and got it home, Aaron, then just fifteen, heard the "ice on the road-no weight in the truck bed" lecture. Our hopes were that he would learn from his older brother's life lesson—ice on the road and no weight in the truck bed demands less speed.

The first real cold snap of the winter two years later brought some snow and freezing rain to our part of central Illinois. Aaron, now seventeen, had horses to feed and water at his grandfather's farm about two miles away. He jumped into the truck and set out to do his evening chores. As he prepared to return to our farm half an hour later, Aaron was aware of the slick road conditions. He buckled his seat belt and headed out of Grandpa's lane going a little slower than usual. After all, "ice on the road-no weight in the truck bed" lectures always had unhappy endings. About a quarter of a mile from our house, Aaron crossed over a bridge. Part two to our driving mantra "ice on the road-no weight in the truck bed" was soon to become "and bridges are even slicker."

As he got onto the bridge, the rear end of the truck slipped to the left. Aaron took his foot off of the accelerator and counter-steered. Now the truck, with a mind of its own, was careening sideways with the bed of the truck in the wrong lane. Thankfully, no one was coming from the opposite direction. The rear end of the truck continued to move to the left and by the time the truck had traveled over the bridge, the rear tires had reached the shoulder and had gotten traction on the gravel.

"Oh good!" you might be saying.

No, actually, "Oh bad!"

Once the rear tires had traction, they sent the truck traveling forward, straight for the ditch. The truck miraculously went through the ditch only to discover the next obstacle. Right in its path was a twenty-foot electric pole. There was no missing it. The collision severed the pole and abruptly stopped the truck.

Amazingly, Aaron was able to get out of the truck and walk to the house. As I recall, upon his arrival Aaron announced that he had some good news and some bad news. The good news was that we all still had electricity and that he was standing there talking to us. (That was *great* news!) And the bad news? Well, that was out in the field.

Aaron now had his own life lesson and through the grace of God he was alive to tell it. That evening (and multiple other times, as I recall) our youngest son, Jonathan, heard the "ice on the road-no weight in the truck bed-icy bridges" lecture. Perhaps he has learned from Aaron's (and Matthew's) life lesson.

Another Life Lesson

An adult woman I know had a life lesson that showed a lot. At the age of fifteen she chose to disobey her parents and sneak around seeing an eighteen-year-old boy. Before long, the foolishness of the decision was obvious as she became pregnant.

I did not meet her until years later—fourteen years to be exact. As we discussed the poor choice she had made and the monumental consequences, she told me about her attempts to insure that her son, born as a result of that choice, would not repeat her pattern. Her hopes were that her life lesson in this area would suffice for both of them.

In this case, I think that it just might, for her child experienced some of the consequences of that poor choice as his mother struggled early on to finish school, hold down a job, and make a home for the two of them. When the child was six, his mother married a kind man who loved them both, adopted the child, and made a secure and loving home for them.

Because her son was six years old before his adopted father entered the picture, he was old enough to remember the consequences both he and his mom suffered because of a foolish choice about sex. And she continues to be quick to remind him. In this case, her life lesson may be adequate for her son also. He will have to make that choice.

Aaron and Miriam's Life Lesson

In the Old Testament we can read of many examples of bad choices and life lessons. One can be found in the twelfth chapter of Numbers. Moses had a brother named Aaron and a sister named Miriam. These siblings helped Moses in his God-given ministry. One day, however, they began to criticize him.

"'Has the Lord spoken only through Moses?' they asked. 'Hasn't he also spoken through us?' And the Lord heard this" (Numbers 12:2).

The Lord not only heard the opposition of Aaron and Miriam, he did not like it. He took action immediately.

At once the Lord said to Moses, Aaron and Miriam, "Come out to the Tent of Meeting, all three of you." So the three of them came out. Then the Lord came down in a pillar of cloud; he stood at the entrance to the Tent and summoned Aaron and Miriam. When both of them stepped forward, he said, "Listen to my words:

"When a prophet of the Lord is among you, I reveal myself to him in visions, I speak to him in dreams. But this is not true of my servant Moses; he is faithful in all my house. With him I speak face to face, clearly and not in riddles; he sees the form of the Lord. Why then were you not afraid to speak against my servant Moses?"

The anger of the Lord burned against them, and he left them.

When the cloud lifted from about the Tent, there stood Miriam—leprous, like snow. Aaron turned toward her and saw that she had leprosy; and he said to Moses, "Please, my lord, do not hold against us the sin we have so foolishly committed."

NUMBERS 12:4-11

Miriam and Aaron made a bad choice—to elevate themselves to the position given only to Moses. This choice angered God, and Miriam suffered severe and immediate consequences. She was given leprosy, a disease so feared its sufferers were shunned by the community.

Aaron took the next step in the life lesson as he pleaded with Moses to intervene on their behalf. Aaron's attitude was genuinely repentant. He had learned from the life lesson.

"Please, my lord, do not hold against us the sin we have so foolishly committed."

Moses cried out to God to heal Miriam. God responded and

she was healed. Their bad choice led to experience and finally the good choice of repentance. It is never again recorded in Scripture that Aaron and Miriam claimed a calling or a relationship with God that was equal to Moses.

"Humble yourselves before the Lord, and he will lift you up" (James 4:10). To be humble is to be teachable. If we will be teachable, God will take our poor choices and turn them into life lessons. If we are not, our poor choices will be to no avail.

God "gives grace to the humble. The wise inherit honor, but fools he holds up to shame" (Proverbs 3:34b-35).

"When pride comes, then comes disgrace, but with humility comes wisdom" (Proverbs 11:2).

Being humble, teachable, and turning foolish choices into experience and life lessons is a very good choice. It is a part of the basic foundation of making choices.

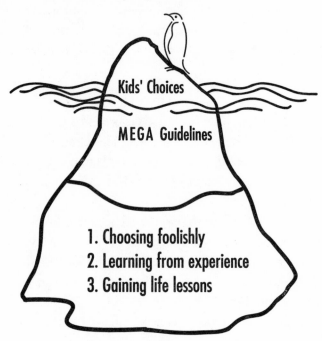

Kids' Choices

MEGA Guidelines

1. Choosing foolishly
2. Learning from experience
3. Gaining life lessons

THREE

Choosing to Blame Others

So then, each of us will give an account of himself to God.

ROMANS 14:12

As we delve further into the universal process of making choices, the foundation for helping your kids make good choices, it is important to examine a poor choice made quite frequently. It is the choice to blame others.

"He made me do it!" That is a common cry of children. When my boys were at the toddler stage and just beyond, they soon learned that using the excuse "He made me do it!" was not effective in our home. In fact, as unusual as it might sound, that was a phrase I didn't allow. You know how that works. You give birth to these delightful and innocent little children and the first time you hear your sweet offspring repeat a word or phrase that is even slightly questionable or offensive, you delete it from the vocabulary of the entire household.

So, in addition to the standard deleted words (I'll let you use your own imagination here) I added the words "He made me do it!" Whenever I heard one of the boys say that, I reminded him that no one made him do anything. His brother (always the "He" in "He made me do it!") may have wanted him to do it. He may have encouraged him to do it. He may have even coerced him into doing it (a different issue to be handled at a later time), but the "doing" was his choice and he would suffer the consequences.

At a conference in Detroit several years ago I mentioned that the phrase "He made me do it!" was not allowed in our home. At that point I pondered (out loud) how our entire nation might be revolutionized in one generation if every mother forbid her children to blame others for their actions and to claim "He made me do it!" At that point, to my great surprise, the audience of about three hundred women burst into applause. They recognized the power that exists in people taking responsibility for their own actions and choosing not to blame others.

Children are not the only ones who say "He made me do it!" As adults, we are much more sophisticated with our accusations and responsibility-dodging. But it all amounts to the same choice—the choice to blame someone else.

"Of course I was late. The jeweler hasn't gotten my watch fixed yet."

"It's not my fault that dinner isn't ready. No one volunteered to pick Sammy up from Cub Scouts."

"I'm so mad at Julie for talking me into taking my little Susie to that birthday party. She didn't feel well and should have stayed home."

We shift the blame. It's not my fault. Someone else is to blame (at least in our own minds) for our poor choices.

This choice, the choice to blame someone else, has been around literally since the beginning of civilization. A quick review of the biblical account of Adam and Eve in the Garden of Eden will set the scene for the first official case of shifting the blame.

The Lord God took the man and put him in the Garden of Eden to work it and take care of it. And the Lord God commanded the man, "You are free to eat from any tree in the garden; but you must not eat from the tree of the knowledge of good and evil, for when you eat of it you will surely die."

The Lord God said, "It is not good for the man to be alone. I will make a helper suitable for him."

So the Lord God caused the man to fall into a deep sleep; and while he was sleeping, he took one of the man's ribs and closed up the place with flesh. Then the Lord God made a woman from the rib he had taken out of the man, and he brought her to the man.

GENESIS 2:15-18, 21-22

Adam and Eve were dwelling together in the most beautiful, lush place ever created. It was filled with "trees that were pleasing to the eye and good for food" (Genesis 2:9). All their needs were met, including their need for communion with God. And as far as we know, there was only one commandment that God had given them to follow. There was only one rule of the road— only one guideline for the garden.

"But you must not eat from the tree of the knowledge of good and evil, for when you eat of it you will surely die" (Genesis 2:17).

Enter the serpent. (Please hear sinister music in the background.) He was determined to twist God's words and confuse the issue. He made the rule more inclusive.

"Did God really say, 'You must not eat from any tree in the garden?'" (Genesis 3:1b).

Unfortunately, the woman didn't have a firm grasp on the exact wording and she added to the confusion. "'...but God did say, "You must not eat fruit from the tree that is in the middle of the garden, and you must not touch it, or you will die"'" (Genesis 3:3). (Who said anything about touching the tree?)

It went from the woman's mild confusion (stimulated by the serpent's bending of the Word of God) to all-out disobedience as the woman actually ate the fruit. Furthermore, she gave some to her husband and he ate it too.

Boy, only one rule to remember ... only one restriction placed by God ... only one opportunity to exercise obedience (or disobedience)—and they couldn't pull it off. Both Adam and Eve made a bad choice.

But wait! Maybe it wasn't really their fault. Sure, neither one could blame their dysfunctional families. (There were no families yet.) And they couldn't attribute their poor choice to their socioeconomic condition. But there still might be a way to claim victim status and officially blame someone else.

First God confronted Adam. "'Have you eaten from the tree that I commanded you not to eat from?'" (Genesis 3:11b). Now that's a pretty direct question. "Adam, did you make a bad choice?" asked God.

Quick, Adam, dodge the direct question. Shift the blame to someone else. Didn't she make you do it? "'The woman you put here with me—she gave me some fruit from the tree, and I ate it'" (Genesis 3:12).

Great work! Even more clever. He was the one who put her here in the first place. It was actually God's fault. Good plan.

And how about Eve? "Then the Lord God said to the woman, 'What is this you have done?' The woman said, 'The serpent deceived me, and I ate'" (Genesis 3:13).

Adam wasn't going to stick her with all the blame. After all, it was the serpent's fault.

"She made me do it!"

"God made me do it!"

"That snake made me do it!"

Choosing to blame someone else has a very long and very illustrious history. And God didn't put much credence in that strategy to dodge personal responsibility even way back then.

To the woman he said, "I will greatly increase your pains in childbearing; with pain you will give birth to children. Your desire will be for your husband, and he will rule over you."

To Adam he said, "Because you listened to your wife and ate from the tree about which I commanded you, 'You must not eat of it,'

"Cursed is the ground because of you; through painful toil you will eat of it all the days of your life. It will produce thorns and thistles for you, and you will eat the plants of the field. By the sweat of your brow you will eat your food until you return to the ground, since from it you were taken; for dust you are and to dust you will return."

GENESIS 3:16-19

Choosing to blame someone else is not a very mature (or acceptable) defense when a bad choice has been made. Nevertheless, it is a popular one.

Beware of Your Words

One simple way we can move toward the elimination of this behavior is to be aware of our language. Just like the child can be encouraged to get rid of the phrase "He made me do it!" we adults can make vocabulary changes too.

Not: "You made me angry by being late."
Instead: "I chose to be angry when you were late."

Not: "I missed the bus because Sally wanted to talk on the phone too long."
Instead: "I missed the bus because I chose to talk to Sally on the phone too long."

Not: "The meatloaf burned because I couldn't hear the timer go off."

Instead: "The meatloaf burned because I chose to work so far from the kitchen that the timer's ring was inaudible. (And I failed to check my watch too.)"

I am a very strong proponent of taking personal responsibility for one's actions. That doesn't mean I always enjoy doing it. I don't always want to accept the responsibility, but I've already mentioned that what we want is not necessarily what is the best, most mature choice. Choosing not to blame others would appear to be the good choice, the godly choice.

"So then, each of us will give an account of himself to God" (Romans 14:12). God doesn't want to hear "He made me do it!"

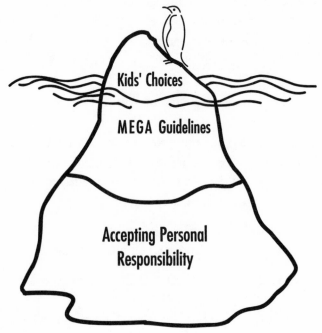

FOUR

Choosing When There Is No Choice

I have learned to be content whatever the circumstances.

PHILIPPIANS 4:11b

How about choosing when there is no choice? Understanding that concept is another part of the foundation for helping your kids make good choices. As a young girl I would try (in vain) to convince my mother that I *had* to do this or that. And invariably she would remind me, "Kendra, there are really only two things you *have* to do—die and pay taxes."

I wouldn't be surprised if many of you heard that same thing from your mothers too. I tried to convince her that I *had* to go ..., or do ..., or have ..., or wear ..., but she really was correct. I had a choice.

There are things, however, that are beyond our realm of choosing. For example, you had no say in your birth order. No one asked you if you wanted your particular birth family (or adoptive family for that matter). You had no choice about the behavior patterns of members of your family (for instance, their choice to love and nurture you or their choice not to). You didn't choose the location of your childhood home or who your neighbors would be. You didn't choose your health or the health of your siblings, parents, or grandparents.

There definitely are circumstances that were and are beyond your control. (Although I think there are fewer than we like to believe.) We cannot control these circumstances, *but* we have control of (and responsibility for) our response to the circumstances.

It's an Old Story

Choosing when there is no choice is not a new concept. This option has existed for centuries. In fact, one of the most well known examples of someone who had no control over many circumstances in his life and yet chose to take responsibility for his response to those circumstances was Joseph from the Old Testament. He could easily be the poster boy for choosing when there is no choice.

Joseph's extenuating circumstances began at an early age. He was his father's favorite son. (No choice of his.) Joseph's brothers did not relish the idea of Joseph having status superior to them. Actually, I'm being much too kind. God's Word says that Joseph's siblings hated him (Genesis 37:4). Again, this was not Joseph's choice.

The brothers acted out their animosity toward Little Joe one day as they dumped him into a cistern to die, then dragged him out and sold him as a slave to a band of Ishmaelites who took him to Egypt. (Joseph once again had no choice. But he will have one before too long.)

Joseph changed hands once again and ended up in the household of Potiphar, an Egyptian official. Now we are told of his choice. He had an opportunity to choose his response to the circumstances. In spite of how things had been going up to that point, he chose to stay connected to God. We all know of people who have chosen to blame God when circumstances were less than attractive. But Joseph's response was not bitterness. Instead he maintained his relationship with the Lord.

Potiphar observed Joseph's response to his circumstances (and God's hand on his life) and rewarded him (Genesis 39:6). Then came the next circumstance beyond Joseph's control. Potiphar's wife chose to proposition Joseph repeatedly (not his choice). And with each proposition came a refusal from Joseph (his choice when there was no choice). "And though she spoke to Joseph day after day, he refused to go to bed with her or even be with her" (Genesis 39:10).

Unfortunately, Joseph had even more opportunities to choose when there was no choice. Potiphar's wife falsely accused him of attacking her and Joseph was sent to prison (Genesis 39:20). Although he did not choose that particular tour of duty, he did choose his response. And again the Lord was with him. Before long Joseph was even proving to be successful in prison as he was put in charge of all those held with him.

Later, while still in prison, Joseph interpreted the dreams of a cupbearer and a baker (Genesis 40). Although the cupbearer promised to put in a good word for him and didn't, Joseph continued to prosper in jail because of his relationship with God.

The entire amazing story of Joseph choosing when there was no choice spans about twenty chapters in Genesis. Joseph was victimized by his family, his friends, and his enemies. Yet he claimed no victim status. He always seemed to be aware of his ability to choose to respond even when there was no choice of circumstances.

In Genesis 45, Joseph spoke to his brothers and shared the precise message of choosing when there is no choice.

I am your brother Joseph, the one you sold into Egypt! And now, do not be distressed and do not be angry with yourselves for selling me here, because it was to save lives that God sent me ahead of you....

So then, it was not you who sent me here, but God. He made me father to Pharaoh, lord of his entire household and ruler of all Egypt.

GENESIS 45:4b-5,8

Joseph chose when there was no choice. He chose to keep his eyes on the Lord and respond with wisdom to his circumstances.

Another Choice

Patricia had always known that she was adopted. Her parents had never kept it a secret. In fact, they told her that after she was eighteen years old they would help her search for her biological family if that was her desire.

She didn't intend to do a search. "In my mind, a search was only done when you didn't like your adoptive parents. And I definitely liked mine."

But the desire to discover answers about her past seemed to escalate as Patricia matured, especially when she took a college course in social work.

"That class dealt extensively with the various issues of adoption and it acted to pique my interest in discovering more about my biological parents. What did they look like? What were their strengths and weaknesses, their likes and dislikes? What were the circumstances of my birth? Where were my biological parents now?"

Patricia talked to her adoptive parents. They hunted through their files and found a paper they had been given when they brought Patricia home. It contained various facts about her biological parents. It told their birthdates, height, weight, and coloring. It described their general health and that of their parents, and listed the number and gender of their siblings. The paper also named several of their interests, some of which Patricia shared. All this information did little to satisfy Patricia's curiosity. Instead, she was stimulated to seek more information.

"Five years after I had first decided I wanted additional information about my biological parents, I met a woman who had founded a search and support group for birth parents, adoptees, and adoptive parents," said Patricia. "This contact, obviously from God, proved to be invaluable."

It was through this woman that Patricia learned about a law on the books in the state where her parents lived during her adoption. It entitled her adoptive parents to certified papers regarding the adoption. These papers were requested and received. With the additional information that the papers provided, Patricia was able to piece the facts together and identify her biological parents. After investing another day or two in research at the public library, Patricia found her biological mother's current name and address. Her birth mother was not married to her birth father.

Now Patricia had to deal with the prospect of contacting her biological mother and possibly creating havoc in her life. (After all, this woman was married and may have never shared this information from her past.) Or possibly the birth mother would not be interested in Patricia's attempt to make a connection.

After much thought and prayer, Patricia wrote to her biological mother and sent the letter by certified mail:

Hello,

My name is Patricia Ann. I was born on March 11, 1974, at 4:15 A.M. at Breakfront Memorial Hospital. I was adopted through the Home Placement Service and I have reason to believe that you are my birth mother.

... I love my adoptive parents dearly and they are both supportive of my search.

... Please know that I do not seek to cause hurt to your family or anyone else, especially you.

In the letter she included her return address and phone number and asked for some acknowledgement if that was possible.

... I would love to correspond with you—maybe even more than that in the future, but I leave that up to you. Please let me know, one way or the other. Receiving no response at all would be worse than a negative response.

Even more importantly, Patricia's letter contained her response to the circumstances of twenty-plus years before—her choice when she had no choice.

... I want to thank you for giving me life. I have no bad feelings toward you, just lots of questions. In fact, I have prayed for you for years. I have had a wonderful life.

Patricia's circumstances? She was the illegitimate daughter of a teenage girl. That was not her choice.

Patricia's response? It was twofold. She had become a Christian when she was in grade school. At that time she had no desire or dream of someday meeting her biological mother.

"I didn't figure we'd ever meet on earth," she said, "but I prayed that someday we would meet in heaven."

Patricia's response was to pray for her biological mother. She was genuinely concerned about the woman's salvation. And in addition to that, when an earthly connection was made, Patricia thanked her mother for giving her life.

You see, Patricia was born one year after abortion was legalized. Her biological mother made a good choice to give her life. Patricia made a good choice in response to circumstances beyond her control. Her responses were prayer and thankfulness. When choosing is not a choice, we can still choose our response. (Patricia's biological mother chose to write back to her, and to this day they have exchanged many letters but have never met as adults. Patricia continues to pray for her salvation.)

You had no choice in the selection of your parents (and your children didn't either). Your mom and dad might have been very disinterested, ill-equipped parents. They might have been abusive, neglectful, or completely absent in your life. That was not your choice or your responsibility. You are only responsible for your response to that circumstance.

Your parents may have been exemplary. They might have provided you with a wonderful, loving home and a positive environment for growth. They may have provided an extraordinary model for your own parenting. They were, however, imperfect. All people, parents or otherwise, fall into that category. And again, you are not responsible for their good or poor behavior. You are responsible for your response to them.

We all have the choice to respond with wisdom and love when there is no choice. And the knowledge that we can choose when there is no choice is a very important aspect in helping your kids make good choices. It is another part of the foundation.

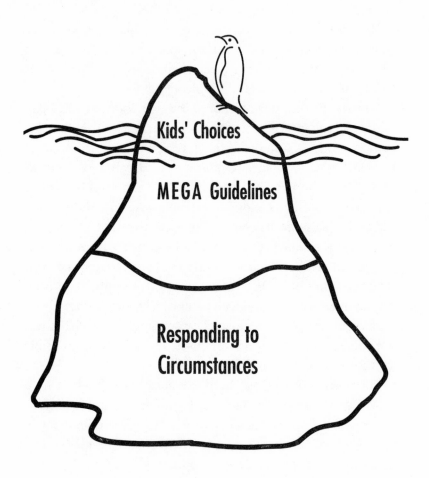

Kids' Choices

MEGA Guidelines

Responding to
Circumstances

FIVE

Choosing Not to Choose

In vain have I washed my hands in innocence.

PSALM 73:13b

We've taken a good hard look at choosing wisely, choosing foolishly, choosing to blame others, and choosing when there is no choice. We have one more aspect of making good choices to examine. There is one more part of the foundation of basic decision making that must be understood in order to help your kids make good choices. That is the concept of choosing not to choose.

You may have never thought of *not* choosing as a choice. Perhaps you merely considered it the polite thing to do or the disinterested alternative.

"Where would you like to go for lunch?"

"I don't care."

"Well, if you're real hungry, we can hit that little smorgasbord on Fifteenth Street. Or if you're not too hungry, we can grab a quick sandwich from the deli."

"Whatever you want."

"Are you hungry for ethnic food? I heard that the new Italian restaurant was pretty good."

"I'm flexible. Whatever."

"OK. Let's head for the sushi bar."

Yikes! Wait a minute. We're not really *that* flexible. We're just trying to get along. We don't want to rock the boat or appear demanding, but *sushi?*

That's a common example of choosing not to choose. We've all been there and done that. We've all given up our privilege of choosing at one time or another. Perhaps the motivation is a genuine attempt to be low maintenance. Perhaps it is the desire to dodge the responsibility attached to choosing. (If the restaurant is bad, it won't be my fault. I didn't choose.)

In reality, choosing not to choose doesn't alleviate the responsibility. It merely gives you the responsibility for "abdicating the throne" and choosing (by default) who will make the decision.

Let me illustrate this concept with a real-life example.

Jenny sat down at the kitchen table to pay the family's monthly bills. Each envelope held approximately what she was expecting until she opened a credit card bill. As Jenny looked over the charges, she was surprised to see a debit to a local motel. "We've never stayed there before," she thought. "Someone must have gotten our account number and charged an overnight."

Unfortunately, Jenny was mistaken. Actually she was half right. *She* had never stayed at that hotel. But her husband and another woman had indeed checked in as the bill correctly indicated.

After Jenny unearthed this information, she was devastated. When her husband Phil arrived home that evening, Jenny confronted him.

Phil seemed to be as upset as Jenny. For the next few days there was very little communication between the two of them. Ultimately Jenny confronted Phil and gave him an ultimatum.

"Phil, after thinking about your actions and spending a lot of time in prayer these past few days," she began, "I've decided that I'm willing to go for counseling. I'll go *if* you choose to immediately stop seeing that other woman. It is me or her. You have to choose."

Phil's reply? "But Jenny, I just can't decide between the two of you."

"Fine," snapped Jenny. "Your choice *not* to decide is answer enough for me. Get out!"

Phil thought he was avoiding making a choice between the two women. In reality, he was just allowing Jenny to make the choice for him. He was still responsible for his choice to commit adultery and for his choice not to change his behavior and go to counseling.

Pontius Pilate's Choice

The biblical personification of choosing not to choose would have to be Pontius Pilate. He was the governor of Judea. Jesus stood before him for questioning after his arrest.

Scripture records that Pilate found no basis for the charges the chief priests and rulers had brought against Jesus.

> You brought me this man as one who was inciting the people to rebellion. I have examined him in your presence and have found no basis for your charges against him. Neither has Herod, for he sent him back to us; as you can see, he has done nothing to deserve death. Therefore, I will punish him and then release him.

> LUKE 23:14-17

Furthermore, Pilate's wife had some input into his decision.

"Don't have anything to do with that innocent man, for I have suffered a great deal today in a dream because of him" (Matthew 27:19b).

His wife had interjected wise counsel. All that was left was to release Jesus as he had said he intended to do. It would seem that Pilate was well on his way to a good choice. He had unemotionally examined the charges and found Jesus innocent.

> Now it was the governor's custom at the Feast to release a prisoner chosen by the crowd. At that time, they had a notorious prisoner, called Barabbas. So when the crowd had gathered, Pilate asked them, "Which one do you want me to release to you: Barabbas, or Jesus who is called Christ?"
>
> MATTHEW 27:15-17

The people cried out for the release not of Jesus, an innocent man, but of Barabbas, a murderer. Pilate did not want to do what the people asked. He did not think it was a good choice.

"Wanting to release Jesus, Pilate appealed to them again. But they kept shouting. 'Crucify him! Crucify him!'" (Luke 23:20-21).

Pilate had ultimate control in the situation. He could have chosen to judge Jesus "not guilty" in spite of the objections of the crowd. But instead he chose not to choose. He relinquished his responsibility.

> When Pilate saw that he was getting nowhere, but that instead an uproar was starting, he took water and washed his hands in front of the crowd. "I am innocent of this man's blood," he said. "It is your responsibility!"
>
> MATTHEW 27:24

He relinquished his authority. He chose to let the crowd have their way, and Jesus was crucified.

"Finally Pilate handed him over to them to be crucified" (John 19:16).

"Surely in vain have I kept my heart pure; in vain have I washed my hands in innocence" (Psalm 73:13).

Pilate's symbolic handwashing did little to relieve him of his responsibility. He knew what was right and he failed to do it. He chose *not* to choose.

The foundation for making good choices involves weighing the pros and cons, seeking wise counsel, evicting the emotions, and learning from life lessons. It also includes taking personal responsibility and responding correctly regardless of the circumstances. In addition we must realize that avoiding a choice does not alleviate the responsibility we have. These are all-important aspects of making choices and the foundation of helping our kids make good choices.

The next section deals specifically with our roles as parents. The principles of making choices that we have examined are universal and apply to young and old alike. These are the base of the foundation. Now we will examine what we can do as parents to help our kids maximize their good choices and minimize their bad choices. This knowledge will give an additional layer to the foundation and act to strengthen the groundwork for our kids' good choices.

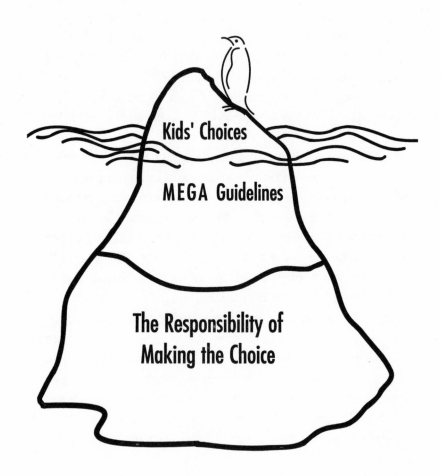

Kids' Choices

MEGA Guidelines

The Responsibility of
Making the Choice

Parents Make Choices— It's Their Opportunity and Responsibility!

He will turn the hearts of the fathers to their children, and the hearts of the children to their fathers.

MALACHI 4:6a

When our older boys were four and two years old (and the youngest son was still unborn) we lived in a tiny home in "downtown" East Lynn. It is necessary for me to put quotation marks around the word downtown because I don't want to lead you astray. The truth of the matter is, there is barely a town much less a downtown.

The population sign says 160 but I have literally counted the people living in East Lynn and have never come up with as many as 160. Perhaps they did the census while someone was having a family reunion. That would explain the inflated number.

Our downtown dwelling was thirty feet by thirty feet with an unfinished attic. That attic was where my husband and I slept. The stairs to our bedroom were very steep. When you were descending, you were eyeball to eyeball with the threshold of the attic floor by step number five.

And it was on the threshold that I tacked a sign. It was rectangular, shaped like a bumper sticker, and simply said, "You are now entering the mission field." I think it was designed to go over the exit door of a sanctuary to remind worshipers that the world outside their church was their mission field.

In our case, however, it was there to remind us that our boys, our family, was our primary mission field. There is great truth and guidance in that reminder.

What kind of mission field has God given you? At that point in our lives, our mission field consisted of two preschoolers. In a couple of years it would expand to three boys. And each year hence it has changed just a little as the boys have matured and our stage of parenting has made adjustments.

Now we have two sons in college and one in high school. The years have passed as quickly as our elders predicted they would. But I have very few regrets, at least fewer than I might have had. Why? I believe it is because of the choice my husband and I made to be intentional in our parenting with God's help. I remember when a friend (the father of a nine-year-old son and three younger children) told us that his oldest child, Craig, was half done. Half done at age nine! Halfway to adulthood and independence.

That statement is a wake-up call. And it can encourage you to choose to be intentional in parenting. But that choice doesn't guarantee complete success. It doesn't presuppose that my kids (or yours) will only make good choices. It can, however, contribute to the commitment that is made to establish a solid foundation upon which they can build their choices.

I don't know where you are today in the ages and stages of parenting, but I do know that the fact that you are reading this book gives evidence to your desire to be intentional in your parenting. You have already committed time and energy to the challenge of helping your kids make good choices.

Being intentional, however, will require more than just reading a book (although that is a good start). As stated earlier, to help our kids make good choices, it takes a certain degree of effort, commitment, and discipline.

Talk-show host Dr. Laura Schlessinger says it well: "Raising children, moral molecule by moral molecule, is very time-consuming, hard work. It requires consistent teaching and discipline, as well as demonstrating goodness by our own actions and interactions."[3]

"Anyone who has raised a child knows it is a tough, challenging, and often frustrating job, interrupted by moments of unsurpassed joy."[4]

Helping our kids make good choices is a hard job with extraordinary rewards. It is worth the effort, commitment, and discipline.

"A wise son brings joy to his father, but a foolish son grief to his mother" (Proverbs 10:1).

After reading (and internalizing) the first section of this book, you have a solid foundation for the basic decision-making process. That is important information to have and is basic to helping your kids make good choices.

Now we will take a little closer look at four guidelines that are specific to parents. These guidelines can assist any parent, regardless of the age and stage of their parenting, to help their kids make good choices.

Years ago it was popular slang to say that one thing or another was not just important, but *mega*-important. The parenting guidelines we will examine to help our kids make good choices are important—*MEGA important*—to add to the foundation of good decision-making skills.

M—MODEL the decision-making process and the making of good choices. It is important for our children to observe us making good choices. They need to see and understand the process that we are going through to arrive at decisions. In addition, they will be able to learn from us as we make poor choices, gain experience, and apply life lessons.

E—ENCOURAGE good choices. Our children need our encouragement to make good choices. That is especially true when a poor choice would seem to be easier than a good choice.

G—GUIDE good choices. Hopefully, our children will seek us out as wise counsel. Then we will have the opportunity to actually guide the decision-making process.

A—ALLOW choices. We must allow our children to make choices. They will make good and bad ones, but the importance of allowing them to fail (as long as that poor choice is not dangerous or life-threatening) cannot be overstressed. It is important for children to practice their decision-making skills while we are still present to help them work through the consequences of a poor choice and gain experience and a life lesson. A parent who does not allow their child to make choices (or to be responsible for the choices made) is doing that child a tremendous disservice.

We will also want to allow our children to develop the God-given talents that they have. We do not want to force our children into areas they are not interested in developing.

In order to examine these MEGA guidelines from different perspectives, I'd like to introduce you to three sets of parents representing three different stages of parenting.

Lisa and Brian

Please meet Lisa and Brian. They have been married for a little over four years. Brian is a high school math teacher and a basketball coach. Lisa received her degree in teaching, but has not had her own classroom up to this point. She was a substitute teacher for several semesters and then became a teacher's aide.

With the new school year approaching, Lisa does not plan on going back to school with the students, for she is pregnant with their first child. She has chosen to be an at-home mom.

Brian and Lisa are both Christians. Lisa accepted Christ as a grade-schooler. She was raised in a one-parent home by a committed Christian mother. Brian became a Christian as a young adult, partially because of the influence of Lisa and her family. Brian's parents were not interested in church or Christ during his formative years.

Since becoming a Christian, Brian has given time and energy to working as an adult advisor to the Fellowship of Christian Athletes huddle in the school where he teaches. Lisa has worked at his side.

Both Brian and Lisa have a strong desire to teach their child God's Word and to instill in him the desire and the ability to make positive decisions. They want to help their kids make good choices.

Joan and Andy

Joan and Andy are at a different stage of parenting. They have two children, ages fourteen and ten. About one year ago, Joan was invited to an informal neighborhood coffee. The woman who extended the invitation mentioned that several women wanted to get together each week to get to know one another better and to discuss issues that touched their lives. She had said something about looking at a biblical view of the issues, but Joan didn't let that bother her. After all, Joan was very open-minded and tolerant. She decided that she would enjoy getting to know her neighbors better as long as the "biblical" part wasn't too extreme.

Joan went the first week and had a very good time. There was a brief prayer before the donuts were served, but nothing offensive in the least.

Actually, the conversation was very uplifting—not filled with the gossip and backbiting that can often be the case when folks gather for coffee. It turned out that three of the five women who met together attended the church at the corner of the park near their homes. Joan had passed it many times and admired its lovely landscaping. She and one other woman had no particular church affiliation (or desire for one), but that didn't seem to bother anyone.

Before they departed that first day, the ladies had determined when and where they would meet the next week. And they decided to read a book on friendship as the catalyst for their discussion. They all agreed to purchase the book and read the first two chapters before they met again.

Joan loved to read and relished the thought of sharing her ideas with others. She had her assignment read within two days.

This pattern continued for many weeks. The women read books on friendship and hospitality and prayer, and all of the books presented a biblical view. It didn't take Joan long to realize that she wanted to know more about the Bible and about Jesus. She and Andy started to attend the church at the corner of the park near their home and they took their kids there too.

Under sound preaching, Joan and Andy both realized their need for a personal relationship with Jesus (see appendix) and they became Christians. This life-changing experience not only affected them and their marriage, but it also impacted their children.

Neal, their oldest child, was fourteen when Joan and Andy decided they wanted to help their children make good choices. Allen, their second-born, was ten. Joan and Andy had not embraced the lifestyle of Christianity or the idea of helping their kids make good choices up to that point in their lives. Now many things were changing. With one child in adolescence and another rapidly approaching that stage, the changes were not necessarily easy for the boys to accept. Nevertheless, the positive choice to help their kids make good choices was worth the effort required.

Ruth and James

Our third couple, Ruth and James, also have two children. Marci is a freshman in college and Christopher is a sophomore in high school. Both Ruth and James have always been nominal churchgoers, with Ruth's attendance records surpassing James. (Big deal: two out of ten Sundays instead of one out of ten.)

As the kids were growing up, Ruth occasionally felt guilty about their lack of commitment when it came to attending church. After all, that was not how she was raised. Her parents had been faithful to their church, their marriage, and their family.

She and James had managed to strike out on all three counts.

Besides a lack of commitment to the church that they had chosen to occasionally attend, she and James had done a pretty poor job of staying interested in their marriage. Likewise, their commitment to their children had been weak.

Ruth's mother lived in the same community and went to the same church. She took the children, Marci and Christopher, to church with her almost every Sunday. Both kids were active in the youth program and even got involved with the music and drama department. Ruth liked her kids being involved. James didn't seem to care one way or the other.

The children were getting solid teaching and even though Marci had told her mother that she had given her heart to Jesus (see appendix), Ruth was not happy. She wished that she were more personally involved in her children's spiritual lives. As a young girl, Ruth had gone forward (see appendix) at church camp and accepted Christ. But she had never nourished that relationship. She desired more involvement with her kids and their spiritual development, but she always argued that it wasn't worth the effort. James' background did not include church and he was usually disinterested and sometimes irritable when Ruth wanted to become more involved. It wasn't worth the effort.

That's what she thought until the summer before Marci left for college. Those three months became very difficult in their home. Marci and her father found themselves in a "knock-down-drag-out" verbal battle almost every night. They fought about curfew and about the cleanliness of her room. They argued about her choice of friends and the use of the car. Their home became a war zone and Ruth began to despair.

With Marci leaving home at the end of the summer, what kind of choices would she make? There would be no one to help her make good choices at college. Grandma wouldn't be picking her up for Sunday school and church each Sunday morning. There was no youth group or drama and music department to provide positive peer pressure and guidance.

The reality of precious time lost was closing in on Ruth, threatening to suffocate her with worry and regret. Could she still help Marci make good choices? Was there time to help her son Christopher?

These three couples will be our hosts as we examine how the MEGA guidelines can be employed at different ages and stages of parenting. No matter where you find yourself today, there is hope and help.

SIX

Choosing to Model the Decision-Making Process and the Making of Good Choices

In everything set them an example by doing what is good.

TITUS 2:7

At this point in their lives, Lisa and Brian have made no mistakes in their parenting. Remember them? They are the young couple expecting their first child. When that child arrives, however, the opportunity will also arrive for Lisa and Brian to become imperfect parents.

But that is not the concern. It is a foregone conclusion that all parents are imperfect. Perfection is not our goal, for that is unattainable. We are instead concerned with focusing on being positive role models for our children in the arena of making choices.

I've heard it said that to be a good role model a person must "walk his talk." I understand the important message. Just talking about things like weighing the pros and cons, seeking wise counsel, and evicting the emotion in making good choices will not be as powerful or persuasive as exemplifying those same keys. Recently, however, I heard someone put an even more realistic, achievable slant on that catchy phrase. Rather than "walk your talk" I was encouraged by the speaker to "stumble my mumble." In other words, do the best I can, however feeble that may be, to be a model for my children. I'm not encouraging you to merely stumble or mumble, I just want to assure you that your effort does not have to be without blemish or fault to make a positive difference in your child's life.

I once heard one of our boys describe my husband by saying, "He always tries to do what is right." He did not say his dad always did what was right. He didn't incorrectly (or unhealthily) claim that John was perfect. Instead he observed his father modeling good choices to the best of his ability.

Being a role model to our children in the art of decision making and modeling good choices is a lot like an activity we all enjoyed in grade school—show-and-tell. You know how it went: You brought your new Tonka truck, the butterfly you caught in the yard, or your baby doll to school. You showed it to your classmates and you told them about it.

Modeling the making of good choices in your children's lives is like show-and-tell. We show the process *and* we explain it. We walk *and* we talk. We stumble *and* we mumble.

"Life skills must be taught. We can't assume that children will learn them just by watching us. Certainly they catch a lot from our example, mostly in the area of values. We vividly illustrate what we value by how we invest our emotions, time, and money. In fact, we cannot *not* model values. But skills must be taught."[5]

Amber's Kids

Amber was a houseparent at a children's home. The kids who lived there were not orphans; they had been removed from their homes because of abuse or neglect. She had ten boys in her cottage, ranging in age from three to twelve. Jim, one of her charges, had been in protective care most of his life. One day he was being especially difficult, causing problems for Amber and for the other boys in their cottage.

Finally, Amber took him aside and tried to talk with him about what was happening. As the conversation progressed, Jim was suddenly flooded with emotion. "You weren't paying attention to me!" he said accusingly. "That's why I was causing trouble. Why didn't you hug me like you were the other boys?"

Amber's answer was that she didn't realize that he needed a hug. She suggested that he tell her when that was the case. "I'm always ready to give you a hug," she explained. "I just didn't know you wanted or needed one. It is always a good choice to let people know what your needs are. Then they don't have to guess. That's what adults do. They tell one another what they need instead of misbehaving to get attention."

The thought that he could choose to express his needs was so completely foreign to him that he was temporarily dumbfounded. When he replied, his answer was simply, "Why didn't my mom ever teach me that?"

As adults, articulating the possible choices and the ones that you *are* making is very important. Telling kids about the process of making choices is also important.

Do we really have to articulate the process and teach our children the art of making good choices? Is it necessary to point out what we are doing as we make choices?

Let's Make a Choice

Years ago I spoke to a group of approximately three thousand junior high student council leaders in the state of Illinois. My message? Making good choices. My avenue for communication? The "Let's Make a Choice" game complete with "valuable cash and prizes behind Door One, Two, and Three and in that large box to the left of the stage!" With lively actions, I taught those three thousand junior high kids the three keys to making good choices: weighing the pros and cons; seeking wise counsel; and evicting the emotion. It was a fun challenge and the students did seem to grasp the concept.

In addition to being the keynote speaker for that convention, I was also the mother of one of the attendees and a driver for some of the students from his school. (Do parents ever wear only one hat?) After the convention was finished late Saturday afternoon, we packed up the vans and headed for home, a six-hour trip.

Included in the various conversations of the return trip was one I had with an eighth-grade girl. She talked to me about my message. This girl was obviously a leader in her school by virtue of her attendance at the convention. She came from a two-parent home where it appeared that the parents were active in their children's lives and made some positive personal choices. In spite of that, this girl marveled at the three basic keys in decision-making that we had dealt with that weekend. She told me she had never heard of those ideas before.

"Weighing the pros and cons, seeking wise counsel, and evicting the emotion makes so much sense," she said. "I've never thought of those before, but now that I have I'm going to remember them and put them to use!"

I was amazed that those three keys were novel to her. Her comments were an illustration that the process of making choices is a skill that can and must be taught. We cannot assume as parents that our kids are aware of the procedure we are using to make good choices. We must model decision making and articulate that process.

Abraham Had a Choice

In God's Word we are given a poignant example of a parent modeling a good choice. In this case it is the choice to be obedient to God and have faith in his Word.

Some time later God tested Abraham. He said to him, "Abraham!"

"Here I am," he replied.

Then God said, "Take your son, your only son, Isaac, whom you love, and go to the region of Moriah. Sacrifice him there as a burnt offering on one of the mountains I will tell you about."

Early the next morning Abraham got up and saddled his donkey. He took with him two of his servants and his son Isaac. When he had cut enough wood for the burnt offering, he set out for the place God had told him about. On the third day Abraham looked up and saw the place in the distance. He said to his servants, "Stay here with the donkey while I and the boy go over there. We will worship and then we will come back to you."

Abraham took the wood for the burnt offering and placed it on his son Isaac, and he himself carried the fire and the knife. As the two of them went on together, Isaac spoke up and said to his father Abraham, "Father?"

"Yes, my son?" Abraham replied.

"The fire and wood are here," Isaac said, "but where is the lamb for the burnt offering?"

Abraham answered, "God himself will provide the lamb for the burnt offering, my son." And the two of them went on together.

GENESIS 22:1-8

God told Abraham what to do and Abraham was prepared to do it. When Isaac questioned the procedure, Abraham answered with complete faith and confidence in God.

At this point we aren't told whether Abraham hoped for a ram in the thicket, or perhaps a resurrection of his beloved son, but we are assured of his obedience to God and his faith in God's Word. Isaac saw that obedience modeled in his father even to the point of Abraham binding Isaac and laying him on the altar he had built. We can only imagine what Isaac was thinking.

Then [Abraham] reached out his hand and took the knife to slay his son. But the angel of the Lord called out to him from heaven, "Abraham! Abraham!"

"Here I am," he replied.

"Do not lay a hand on the boy," he said. "Do not do anything to him. Now I know that you fear God, because you have not withheld from me your son, your only son."

GENESIS 22:10-12

After the angel stopped Abraham, a ram caught by its horns in a thicket was provided for the burnt offering. Abraham was obedient once again as he sacrificed the ram. (I can imagine that his obedience might have been even more enthusiastic this time.) And Isaac saw his father modeling obedience and heard his father declare that God would provide.

The biblical example is unique. Lisa and Brian, our young couple expecting their first child, will not be asked to model obedience to God in the same way Abraham was asked. But they will have many opportunities to teach their child, by modeling, how to make good choices. Because they are just beginning the adventure of parenthood, they will have teachable moments at every stage of their child's life.

Brian and Lisa's attendance in worship each week is an important choice to model and in many ways reflects their relationship with God and their obedience to him. We know that attending worship is a good choice because God's Word encourages us to "forsake not the assembling of yourselves together" (Hebrews 10:25, KJV). Their newborn will not question this choice. Infants are not capable of making or questioning choices. When the child matures and asks why they attend church each week, Lisa and Brian will be able to present the all-important "pro" of being obedient to the Word of God. The Word is also wise counsel. Evicting the emotion is illustrated when church attendance is chosen even when (for whatever reason) Lisa or Brian don't want to go. Lisa and Brian will be modeling a good choice.

In contrast, if they find an excuse for absence, other than illness, their child will see the model of "convenient worship" rather than "committed worship." The child will learn that some things are more important than worship—like preparing dinner when a crowd is coming or finishing up the lawn before a big storm. Later in life, their child may not use these exact excuses, but he will have learned that there are things that

preempt worship. Maybe he is too tired after a big football vic-
tory on Saturday night. Or perhaps he has scheduled an outing
with friends that begins before worship ends. If worship is
important to Lisa and Brian and they desire for their child to
make the good choice to make worship important in his life,
they must do more than just say the words. They must show it
with their habits and their lives.

As a preschooler, Lisa and Brian's child will follow their lead
in interacting with others. If they model the choice to be criti-
cal of others and not to encourage others, that choice will be
easier for their child to make. God calls us to be encouragers, so
that is the good choice. "Therefore encourage one another and
build each other up" (1 Thessalonians 5:11a).

The choices that Lisa and Brian make in the way they treat
one another will be another model for their child. We make
daily decisions in regard to our relationships with other people.
Lisa and Brian's child will make choices too. What are the positives of husbands and wives treating one another with respect?
We are instructed to do so in God's Word. "Each one of you
also must love his wife as he loves himself, and the wife must
respect her husband" (Ephesians 5:33). And God's Word is
always wise counsel! Treating one another with courtesy,
respect, and love does not mean Lisa and Brian will never dis-
agree. It will be their choice whether or not to extend love,
courtesy, and respect even when they are angry or provoked. If
they choose to do this, they are modeling a good choice for
their child.

The choices Lisa and Brian make in their vocabulary will also
be a model for the choice their child will make. "Out of the
overflow of the heart the mouth speaks" (Matthew 12:34b).
The words we speak can reveal a great deal about our character.

At a recent high school football game, a group of students sat near enough to my husband and me that we could hear their conversation and yet far enough away for them to forget that we were present. At one point a young man (I can't say "young gentleman"; I'd be lying) spewed forth a sentence or two of complete filth. I made a mental note of him as "one to be avoided in the friendship circle" unless major changes occurred in his life. His mouth gave him away. I wonder what kind of talk he hears at home—or do I?

Like Parents, Like Child

As a former elementary school teacher, parent-teacher conferences in the fall of the year were very telling. As I met the parents of little Johnny or Sally, I quickly knew where the child had learned to use poor grammar. Or worse, where they had learned their "colorful" language. Modeling is powerful.

Lisa and Brian will constantly be modeling choices regarding the physical and health issues of life also. The pattern of eating their child develops will begin in their home. Lisa and Brian will have opportunities to model good choices about nutrition, exercise, and the use, nonuse, or misuse of drugs, alcohol, and tobacco.

My husband's parents had made the choice as young adults not to smoke. At that time there was very little information about the potential health risk involved in smoking. Years later, when they were raising their family, research began to reveal some of the dangers related to smoking.

My in-laws had an ingenious way beyond modeling to communicate to their children the good choice they hoped their children would make. When they read a newspaper or magazine article about the perils of smoking, they shared it with their kids. When the kids read the information for themselves, they were getting the facts from an independent, unbiased source and it made an impact.

My mother- and father-in-law were providing their children with adequate information to weigh the pros and cons and make a good choice not to smoke. They were personally modeling and advocating that choice, and the experts in the articles also functioned in the capacity of wise counsel. By eliminating any lectures on the evils of smoking, there was very little emotion to evict. Success! Not a smoker in the crew. Lisa and Brian could model positive health choices in this manner too.

As parents we also have the opportunity to model positive choices in intellectual development. Lisa and Brian will have opportunities to continue to learn by reading and listening and sharing ideas. They can model this behavior or they can choose to be stagnant in their intellectual growth. Their choices are likely to be mimicked by their child. If the TV is not on during dinner but instead the family visits about the day with its delights and disappointments and its moments of learning, this behavior will become the pattern. Relationships will also be enhanced.

Undoubtedly Lisa and Brian will have the opportunity to model life lessons for their child. These are lessons they gain from poor decisions. Perhaps the most important and meaningful model of a life lesson will occur when Lisa and Brian make a bad choice in relationship to their child. That poor choice will give them some wonderful opportunities. They will have the chance to admit to their child that they made a mistake and made a bad choice. Then they will be able to say "I'm sorry" and ask for forgiveness. And finally Lisa and Brian will be able to model that all important "change in behavior" that comes from a life lesson.

Quantity Versus Quality

Modeling good choices and the process of decision making takes time and effort. When my children were young, there was a very popular argument among parenting experts. The debate was "quantity time versus quality time."

"Don't worry about how much time you spend with your child," some experts touted. "Merely strive for quality time when you are together."

In my opinion, that attitude created a phenomenal amount of stress on most parents. First of all, it encouraged them to spend the majority of their time in an endeavor other than parenting, adding increased responsibility to their already overbooked lives. Then it demanded that the miniscule amount of time the parent invested in the child's life *must* be quality time. The pressure was overwhelming. Have you ever tried to make each interaction, each meeting with someone, a moment of quality?

Personally, I have decided that the answer to the quality time versus quantity time debate is as follows: Quality time is something that occasionally happens while you are busy having quantity time. As Lisa and Brian spend time with their child, they will be able to look for those glimpses of quality time and grasp them.

Lisa and Brian will have to be committed to their goal of helping their child make good choices and will have to exercise godly disciplines in their own lives. Their behavior, the model they present, is an important part in helping their child make good choices. And being consistent in modeling is an important parenting principle.

Never Too Late

Joan and Andy have a different set of circumstances when it comes to both modeling good decision-making skills and the making of good choices. Unfortunately, they did not begin the process of making godly choices themselves until recently. Now they also want to help their kids learn how to do it. Even though their sons are used to the old pattern of behavior, it is not too late for a change.

Because Joan and Andy's sons are older (ten and fourteen; both over "half done") the idea of show *and* tell is perhaps even more important. First of all, their children are old enough to understand completely the explanation of why certain choices are being made today that had not previously been made.

For example, prior to making a commitment to Christ, Joan and Andy drank alcohol to excess each weekend and occasionally in mid-week too. This was the choice they modeled for their children. After their conversion, both Joan and Andy realized that this behavior was destructive and that their alcohol consumption had most definitely not been in moderation. Because they felt strongly about their desire not to fall into old habits again, Joan and Andy chose to completely abstain from drinking alcoholic beverages. In fact, they removed all the liquor from their home. Their sons were well aware of this radical change and were able to listen to and understand how their parents made this choice. Joan and Andy weighed the pros and cons of drinking to excess and found many cons and not a single pro. They sought wise counsel from their pastor and their physician. And they evicted the emotion in regard to this issue. In this case, the emotion was the desire to repeat the old habit and the ease with which that could be done. They made a good choice in regard to their health and they modeled it for their boys.

This is only one example of the change that occurred in their household. Sunday, which had always been a day of late brunch and lazy lounging, became a day spent at the church at the corner of the park near their home. They began to attend both morning and evening services. Joan and Andy desired to grow in their relationship with God and to give their sons the opportunity to do likewise. They made this good choice. They modeled it with their actions and also explained the change to their sons.

Before the change in Joan and Andy's hearts, home, and behavior, a phone call to their home in the evening brought a very predictable poor choice.

Rrrring! Rrrring! "Honey," Andy would holler, "if that's for me, tell them I'm not home. I'm too tired to take one more call."

And Joan would do precisely what Andy requested. She would answer the phone and if the caller asked for Andy, she would say he wasn't home. She would lie.

When Joan and Andy started making life changes (and modeling those for their children), they both realized that the "phone routine" was something that would have to change. They had been making a bad choice to model deceit to their kids. As Christians, they wanted that to change.

Rrrring! Rrrring! "Yes, Andy's here," Joan now answered, "but he's resting. Would I be able to help you or can I take a message?"

More honest. More correctly modeling the character of God and his people.

Joan and Andy also changed the type of reading material they preferred and in so doing they improved the model they presented to their boys. Gone were the questionable magazines and videos. Now Joan and Andy spent time filling their minds with knowledge about God and his Word. They discovered Christian cable channels on the television that they never knew existed and began to faithfully read and study the Bible. They had previously been modeling the practical computer-age phrase ... garbage in, garbage out. And now they modeled the converse—good things in, good things out. They made it a priority to put good things into their minds. "Do not conform any longer to the pattern of this world, but be transformed by the renewing of your mind" (Romans 12:2a). They modeled this choice, this positive decision, for their children.

Furthermore, Joan and Andy modeled a change of behavior in how they treated one another. When hurtful words were no longer pouring out onto the domestic battlefield, the battles soon stopped. Instead of using their mouths for cursing, they were used for edification. "A word aptly spoken is like apples of gold in settings of silver" (Proverbs 25:11). They modeled this new behavior and their relationship modeled the positive results.

There were many changes in Joan and Andy's lives. Change itself is difficult for people. And the multiple changes in the lives of the two people who sons Neal and Allen thought they had "all figured out," was somewhat confusing. These boys determined that their parents' explanations of all their newly established behaviors would not be enough. The boys decided to scrutinize their parents and looked for holes in their rationale and their behavior. Needless to say, they wouldn't look for mistakes or poor choices in vain. Inevitably Joan and Andy will make a bad choice. When that happens, it will be very important for them to admit the mistake as soon as it is realized. When the boys see a life lesson in action, they will be even more convinced that the change in their parents is not merely temporary.

In order for Joan and Andy to model making positive choices for their kids, they know they will have to be diligent in their new way of life and they will have to be consistent. Fluctuating between the new and old behaviors will only reinforce the old way of life and convince their children that the chance exists to return to the more comfortable, predictable past. Vacillating will make it more difficult for their boys to emulate the positive model.

Again, we must remember that undoubtedly Joan and Andy will fail more than once. That's guaranteed. But a poor choice is not a disaster. It is merely an opportunity for experience and a life lesson.

Consistency will be important for Joan and Andy. In addition to being consistent, they must also be persistent. It is *never* too late for a change. In their stage of parenting, it can be more difficult. It is not, however, impossible.

Joan and Andy's boys were both over "half done" when the parents made the decision to help them make good choices. These two young men are intellectually ready to understand the importance of the three keys to making good choices and to understand the painful positives of a life lesson. That is very helpful. They are, however, used to the old patterns. The challenge is real, but the results are worth the effort, commitment, discipline, and changes in behavior. Joan and Andy have decided to help their kids make good, godly choices, and they are willing to accept the challenge.

> While it's preferable to "train a child in the way he should go," a new window of opportunity could arrive in the midst of present conflict ... the eye of the storm. Make no mistake; there's no foolproof formula for renewal. Each situation is different. But with prayer, love and sensitivity, it's never too late to reverse patterns of poor decision making.[6]

Nothing Is Impossible

Ruth and James have the most difficult situation. Their daughter, Marci, has just gone to college and their son, Christopher, is already in high school. Is it too late for them to model the decision-making process and to model the making of good choices? The answer is no, but the importance of being consistent and persistent are magnified even more. Ruth, even if she alone desires to help her kids make good choices, will have to live the positive life changes of that desire. Because Marci is gone, Ruth will have only limited opportunities to model the art of decision making and the making of good choices. She will, however, have some opportunities.

Unfortunately, it would seem that James does not share Ruth's desire to help their kids make good choices. Although that is sad, the truth is that Ruth is not responsible for James nor can she control him. She is responsible for her own behavior and the choices she makes.

One other factor that definitely complicates the issue of Ruth and James making good choices is the seesaw behavior that has been their previous life pattern. They have been on again-off again in church attendance and other areas of commitment. If Ruth alone or Ruth and James want to model the making of good choices, they will have to become very consistent in their positive choices. They do not have the luxury of an unstable behavior pattern. Their previous behavior, intermittently reinforcing poor choices, has definitely strengthened the influence of those bad choices.

Parents who never attended church and then change completely to become regular attendees (like Joan and Andy) will actually find it easier to extinguish the original poor choice of not attending worship. The pattern of Ruth and James, sporadic church attendance, and only occasional interest in their children's choices, is much more difficult to defeat. Are Ruth and James simply toying with a change? Will the change be sporadic and occasional like all the others? In order for their kids to identify a positive change, it will have to be very consistent, leaving almost no room for deviation.

How can Ruth and James model these positive choices? Assuredly, Christopher will see the positive change with more frequency than Marci, but even occasional exposure to the change will be good. If Ruth and James have a true desire to help their kids make good choices, they can make a difference by modeling.

First of all, Ruth and James or Ruth alone can choose to become committed to worship. Christopher is already going to church regularly with Grandma and regardless of what her husband, James, chooses, Ruth can choose to go. Undoubtedly, there are learning opportunities provided by the church such as

Sunday school and perhaps a Bible study. Becoming involved in those would definitely model positive choices in the realm of spiritual and intellectual growth.

Looking for ways to develop and improve the relationship with her son, Christopher, would also be a positive choice. The old activities of his childhood will obviously not be applicable, but Ruth can be creative and structure new relationship-building times. Perhaps James will want to make these positive choices too.

Ruth's habit of comparing herself to her husband and rating herself spiritually superior will have to come to an end, too. Our plumb line for behavior is not one another, it is Christ. The more Ruth learns about the Lord, the more her character will reflect his. That is always a good choice.

As far as choices in the arena of our physical being, the majority of Ruth and James' choices have been healthy ones up to this point. Those choices probably do not need to change. They may find that they will have opportunities to express (especially to Christopher) the whys of their choices and model the decision making process.

Ruth and James will have to be persistent in their communication and in their positive choices. Because the whole concept of helping their kids make good choices came at such an advanced stage of parenting, the rigors of commitment, behavior, discipline, and effort are more demanding for Ruth and James.

This couple has an uphill struggle in helping Marci and Christopher make good choices, but uphill isn't impossible. It just requires that they be more consistent and more persistent. And, in addition, they will also have to be resistant—resistant to the world as it calls with its familiar cry of "Give up! You're defeated! You can't make a difference by modeling good decision making."

God encourages us never to feel or say or think or act on the premise that it is too late to make a difference. Remember the Israelites after they left Egypt? Pharaoh was in hot pursuit of the Israelites with "all [his] horses and chariots, horsemen and troops" (Exodus 14:9b).

> As Pharaoh approached, the Israelites looked up, and there were the Egyptians, marching after them. They were terrified and cried out to the Lord. They said to Moses, "Was it because there were no graves in Egypt that you brought us to the desert to die? What have you done to us by bringing us out of Egypt? Didn't we say to you in Egypt, 'Leave us alone; let us serve the Egyptians'? It would have been better for us to serve the Egyptians than to die in the desert!"
>
> EXODUS 14:10-12

They didn't have the big picture, did they? Moses knew that God had a plan for deliverance and he reassured the people. "'Do not be afraid. Stand firm and you will see the deliverance the Lord will bring you today'" (Exodus 14:13a). Don't give up yet! It may seem impossible, but we're not defeated. Pay attention. It's not over till the fat lady sings. And she's not even warming up yet.

And with that, God gave Moses instructions for the parting of the Red Sea and the Israelites crossed on dry land. Wow! That's some deliverance! Don't give up too soon. (And it's almost always too soon.)

Ruth and James can also appreciate that Marci, technically an adult, is also a Christian. She accepted Christ and they have the wonderful assurance that he is with her guiding her. He is the best guide and model that any parent could hope for. Not only is he the wisest, but he is ever present.

Ruth and James' assignment to choose to model the decision-making process and the making of good choices and to respond to bad choices by gaining experience and obtaining a life lesson is not an easy one. But the options are either to: (1) begin today and make a difference to one degree or another in Marci's life and even more probably in Christopher's life; or (2) wait another three years and send Christopher to college lamenting the loss of the opportunity to help him make good choices. Ruth, with or without James, must begin *now* to model positive choices for her children.

In fact, the message of urgency is not just one for Ruth and James. Each day provides an opportunity to reinforce, by our behavior, by modeling, the principles of positive decision making and the benefits of life lessons.

What are you waiting for? Today is the right time to begin regardless of your stage of parenting. Model godly decisions by weighing the pros and cons, seeking wise counsel, and evicting the emotion. Be sure to *show and tell* the process. Don't be discouraged with your inability to be the perfect model, instead when a poor choice is made, turn it into experience and a life lesson. And share that with your children. That will reassure them that there can ultimately be a good choice made even when a poor choice has been made first.

Modeling the decision-making process and the making of good choices will add another layer of strength to the foundation. It will help your kids make good choices.

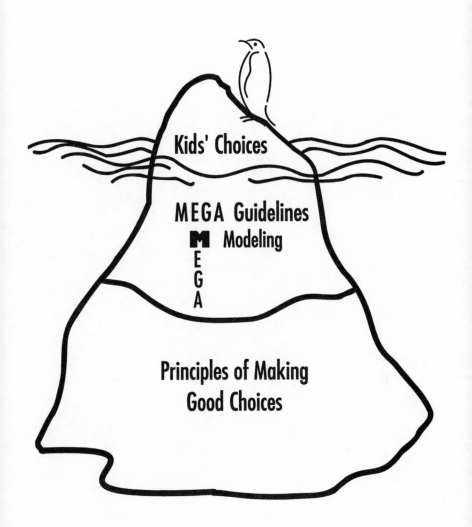

SEVEN

Choosing to Encourage Good Choices

But encourage one another daily, as long as it is called Today, so that none of you may be hardened by sin's deceitfulness.

HEBREWS 3:13

Good choices are not always easy choices. Occasionally they are very difficult. Good choices are not always the choices we *want* to make. Sometimes poor choices have more appeal. Good choices are not always the most pleasant, but they are always the best.

One of our assignments as parents, and another layer of the MEGA guidelines foundation, is to encourage our children to make good choices. This adds to the base of support they will have for making good choices.

Encouragement is a very important and very powerful motivator. God instructs us multiple times in his Word to be encouragers.

"Therefore encourage each other with these words" (1 Thessalonians 4:18).

"Therefore encourage one another and build each other up, just as in fact you are doing" (1 Thessalonians 5:11).

The Word also tells us of God's role as an encourager. "You

[the Lord] encourage them and you listen to their cry" (Psalm 10:17b).

We can see that encouragement is a very good, biblical choice. It is important to note that encouragement is not simply cheering someone's accomplishments. We tend to think of it in that way.

"Good job on your Sunday school memory verses."

"Congratulations on the A+ on your spelling test."

"You did a great job at the ball game."

Applauding performance or outcome is certainly one very important aspect of encouragement. But in our pursuit to help our kids make good choices, we are specifically dealing with encouraging good choices regardless of the outcome.

"That was a good choice you made to spend some time each day this week learning your memory verses." (Even if the child failed to say each verse perfectly on Sunday morning. The choice was a good one.)

"You made a good choice to write out the spelling words as practice for your test." (Again, an A+ is not necessary for us to give encouraging words.)

"Your good choice to practice shooting free throws really paid off at the ball game." (The good choice, rather than the scoring, is encouraged here.)

What good choices are being encouraged by those statements? We are encouraging discipline, practice, and planning ahead. Those are good choices in many areas of life, not just memorization, spelling, and sports. They are definitely to be encouraged.

Too many times we encourage and applaud the outcome and not the process or the choices that may have led to the outcome. Have you ever seen a poorly executed free throw (no stable base, no square stance, no follow-through) that actually goes through the hoop? Of course you have. We all have. That poorly executed shot scores one point just like the picture perfect shot that is made. It is, however, not technically a good shot. Likewise, a technically superior shot (good footing, square to the basket, complete follow-through) may on occasion not go through the hoop. It is not a bad shot. The coach or parent who hollers "great shot" just because a point is scored is only applauding the outcome. The technically accurate shot is actually the "great shot" and will ultimately go through the hoop many more times than the poor shot. This shooter has made the choice to practice the basics for a great shot.

The child who does not study his spelling words, peeks at his neighbor's paper, and gets an A+ on the spelling test has not done a great job. His choices were poor even though he "scored" on the outcome. If we only applaud performance, in this case, we are actually encouraging a poor choice.

We want to encourage the truly great shot—the good choice to execute, in the first example, a free throw with precision and good form. We want to encourage the choice that occurred long before the shooter went to the line. We want to encourage his good choice to practice the skill correctly.

We want to encourage the child who studies his spelling with diligence. We want to encourage the one who does his own work and does not cheat by looking at his neighbor's paper. We want to applaud his good choices. The chances are the outcome will also reflect the good choice.

It is important to encourage "with great patience and careful instruction" (2 Timothy 4:2). This piece of advice from God's Word that emphasizes patience will help us to encourage the good choices and not merely the performance. The choices of diligence and of practice are good choices and will many times lead to good performance. Then we can applaud both!

Sometimes, perhaps even innocently, parents do not choose to encourage their kids to make good choices. Instead they do just the opposite and encourage poor choices.

Isn't He Cute?

In my years of teaching school, I saw more than one example of parents encouraging their children to make poor choices. Sometimes the poor choices were viewed as cute or clever. Sometimes they were viewed as harmless. Typically they were ultimately not cute, clever, or harmless, but instead were the beginning of a pattern of making poor choices.

Sam was the baby in the family. Everyone thought he was just as cute as a button since he first arrived on the scene. His father, especially, encouraged his precocious behavior and rewarded his ability to dodge responsibility with cleverness and cunning. Sam was seldom disciplined even though his behavior warranted it. When he began school, he immediately assumed the role of class clown. The kids laughed at his antics and although the teacher encouraged more mature behavior and met with his parents on numerous occasions, Sam's family continued to applaud his misbehavior.

By the time Sam reached my classroom, he was very far behind in the basic skills, although he was obviously of above average intelligence. He had joked, charmed, and conned his way around homework assignments and learning opportunities for years and now he was far behind in the necessary skills.

Sam and I worked very hard that school year to bring him up

to a level slightly below average. Actually, for the first half of the year, I worked hard at that and he worked hard at avoiding me and avoiding responsibility for his consistently poor performance. By mid-semester, he began to realize the price he was paying (and worse yet, the price he would continue to pay) if he chose to keep being irresponsible in his schoolwork as he had been for so many years.

His parents also began to see that Sam's irresponsibility was now demanding a high price. As we met together to begin to form a strategy to help Sam escape from the deep hole of poor performance he had climbed into, his father made a very insightful and somewhat melancholy observation.

As we talked about how Sam would have to choose to change his attitude about school and learning, Sam's dad gave me a mournful glance and said, "I always used to think it was so cute. I guess it's not so cute anymore."

The "it" he was referring to was Sam's clever misbehavior. And Sam's dad was right—it was not so cute anymore. It was sad for me to realize that up until that moment in time, Sam's disruptive behavior *had* been viewed as cute and had been encouraged. It would have been much easier for Sam if his parents had wanted to encourage him to make good choices from a much earlier time in his life.

We do not want to convince ourselves that encouraging poor choices doesn't really matter. It is important to be intentional in our parenting. The parents that laughingly give their preschooler a cigar and a bottle of beer or encourages him to spit, kick, hit, or say naughty words, will find out very soon that "it isn't so cute anymore."

Lisa and Brian

Looking once again at our three couples, Lisa and Brian have the advantage of being able to choose to encourage their child to make good choices from the very beginning of his life. Let's look at some of the areas where good choices can be encouraged and some of the avenues for that encouragement.

Lisa and Brian will undoubtedly be found encouraging their child to take his first steps and say his first words. Almost every parent gladly assumes these tasks. That is encouraging his performance and is certainly not to be overlooked. Even more important, though, is encouraging those good choices.

If their little child chooses to pull back his hand when he is told not to touch the plant in the corner, Lisa and Brian can applaud this good choice and good behavior. "Good boy. That's a good boy to mind Mommy and Daddy."

These words of encouragement will motivate him to be obedient. A child who learns to be obedient to his parents will find being obedient to God less difficult. Lisa and Brian will have occasions to encourage obedience to God and to his Word. They can encourage their child to learn what God's Word says. This can be accomplished by encouraging and applauding attendance at Sunday school and church each week and by dialoging about the lessons that are taught.

In addition, Lisa and Brian can have a time of family devotions. This doesn't have to be a somber gathering, but instead can be fun and employ object lessons where Scripture is read and applied.

When our kids were growing up we had a time of family devotions each morning. There was nothing particularly holy about choosing the morning time, it simply worked best for us.

From the beginning we had three underlying objectives for the devotion time. (1) We wanted the boys to truly understand that God was good. We wanted them to know the nature of God by knowing his Word. (2) We wanted them to know that God loved them, and that his love exceeded even the love we had for them. (3) We wanted them to know that God desired the very best for them. These goals were pursued by having a relaxed time together each morning when we shared a Bible story or a Bible truth and an application to their lives.

Our family devotional time was not a serene and deeply spiritual moment with all heads bowed and all hands folded. No, it was what I fondly refer to as devotion commotion. The boys ate their breakfast as their dad or I read to them. They shuffled and squirmed and interjected ideas as they popped into their heads. The Word of God was being spoken in spite of the sometimes noisy setting.

In John 14:26 Jesus tells us that "'the Counselor, the Holy Spirit, whom the Father will send in my name, will teach you all things and will remind you of everything I have said to you.'" Oswald Chambers, in his book *The Moral Foundations of Life* (1966), built on this. "The Holy Spirit cannot bring back to our minds what we have never troubled to put there." I always felt confident that we were putting the Word of God into the boys' minds and hearts during those casual morning sessions.

Each morning we ended our time together holding hands in prayer, and after the "amen" I often heard comments like "He had his eyes open!" (Think about that one for just a minute. The accuser signed his own admission of guilt by making the accusation.) We never scolded or demanded perfect attention or punished the boy (or two) who had his eyes open. Instead, devotion time was a pleasant time of hearing the Word and finding application to their lives through a story. Sometimes we worked as a family on memorizing a verse of Scripture. Sometimes (especially as the boys got older) we talked about how the application we had just read could be adapted to create a great children's sermon. Always we ended in prayer for the day. In fact, our breakfast meal has almost never begun in prayer. This particular routine gave each family member the freedom to assemble together at their own pace and start eating their breakfast while it was still hot. (Dad was and is a short-order breakfast cook.) Our tradition was to end the meal and start the day with prayer. (I'd sometimes forget to tell the occasional overnight visitor about our system and they would watch in horror as the boys dug into their scrambled eggs or French toast without a blessing.)

Our plan was not perfect. It was not the *only* way to conduct family devotions, but it worked for us. Lisa and Brian will have to establish a plan that works for them. There are excellent resources that are available to help families achieve their goals for daily devotions or family nights.

Lisa and Brian can also encourage their child by praying with him. Saying bedtime prayers is a wonderful way to encourage the good choice of communicating with God. When our boys were young we led their prayers for family and friends. Then they entered school and we added teachers and assignments. Finally we were praying for ball games and ultimately we left them on their own to speak with God at the end of the day.

One of my fondest memories of each of my sons' younger years is the finish to those prayers of early childhood and grade school. At the end of each bedtime prayer we would say, "Mom and Dad love you lots and lots. And who loves you best of all?" "Jesus!" they would reply, as much from habit as from conviction, but you can be sure they knew the answer to the question that we asked daily. Again a reinforcement of one of our goals—to help them understand God's overwhelming love for them.

Lisa and Brian can develop their own rituals and routines that will encourage their child to make the good choice to read God's Word, apply it to his life, and pray.

As Lisa and Brian observe their child interacting with others, they will have ample opportunities to encourage good choices in interpersonal relationships. As they observe simple behavior such as sharing with others, they will be able to applaud that choice.

Lisa and Brian can encourage good choices in the arena of the physical also. Our bodies are the "temple of the Holy Spirit" (1 Corinthians 6:19) and it is a good choice to maintain a healthy body. When their child chooses a healthy snack such as fruit instead of soda pop, Lisa and Brian will be able to encourage that choice. They can encourage participation in activity as opposed to a sedentary pastime. Playing outdoors in the fresh air is almost always a superior choice to sitting in front of the television or computer. By reading good books to their child, Lisa and Brian will encourage his interest and enjoyment in reading.

One final point before we leave Lisa and Brian in their pursuit of encouraging their child to make good choices. In the early stages of life, we encourage good choices by literally making good choices *on behalf of* our child. A preschooler can be told that it is time to turn off the TV and get the ball for a game of catch. That order is encouraging a good choice. The child is not old enough yet to be left to his own in all cases of decision making.

In a sense, when our kids are young, we can demand a good choice. Lisa and Brian will want to do that initially and then transition from the controlling demand to encouragement as their child matures. Encouragement is not demanding. It is much more like positive motivation. We can encourage our kids when a good choice is made and even as they contemplate that choice. That is positive interaction. Demanding they make a good choice after they are old enough to decide for themselves, does not accomplish the same thing over the long run.

Encouraging kind words to another child is not forcing your child to speak in one way or another. Encouraging empowers your child to make a good choice. Demanding controls his choice. Applauding and encouraging the choice in snack food influences your child to continue to make that good choice. Controlling the snack food choice merely eliminates his choice for the moment. Always remember that our goal is to help our kids make good choices and to model and encourage good choices.

Lisa and Brian will want to encourage their child first by choosing wisely for him and then by gradually allowing him to choose for himself. Encouraging good choices is another layer of the strong foundation which can help our kids make good choices.

Joan and Andy

Joan and Andy have a little different circumstance because they are not starting with a clean slate. Their children, Neal and Allen, have not always been encouraged to make good choices. Before their parents' conversion, the boys operated under different standards and beliefs. Being encouraged to make good choices was not an important part of their lives. Now things have changed.

How can Joan and Andy make this adjustment and encourage their boys to make good choices? They have realized that before they knew Christ they had only done this infrequently. Instead, Joan and Andy had been interested entirely in the outcome—in the performance of their children. If Neal caught the pass, he was applauded and sometimes even rewarded with a fast food stop after the football game. If he missed the pass, he was scolded and questioned about his commitment to the game of football. There were no milkshakes after a poor performance game. And there was very little love, acceptance, and approval communicated.

That was before. Now Joan and Andy knew that things needed to change. They wanted to encourage Neal regardless of the outcome of his performance. At one particular football game, Neal was on the sidelines for a play and the quarterback threw a long pass to another receiver. The receiver caught the ball and scampered into the end zone for a touchdown. As the receiver ran off the field, Neal ran toward him, giving him a high five and congratulating him on his great reception and run. Joan and Andy had a wonderful opportunity to encourage and applaud a good choice.

"I saw you cheering for Bill as he caught that pass in the third quarter. I know that it made him feel good that you were excited for him."

In my gift book *It's A Mom Thing!*, I said it this way …

Moms are cheerleaders. They cheer their children when they succeed. They cheer up their children when they don't succeed. And perhaps more importantly, they cheer their children as their children cheer those who succeed and cheer up those who don't succeed.[7]

Cheering our kids' good choices is even more important than cheering their accomplishments. Joan and Andy will have to look for opportunities to encourage good choices reflecting good character in their children.

Because Neal and Allen have not always been encouraged to make good choices, there is a little "undoing" to be done. Unfortunately, Joan and Andy have inadvertently encouraged Allen to make poor choices.

Allen's performance, not just Neal's, had always been the only thing his parents applauded. Joan and Andy had never seemed to care *how* the outcome was achieved, they merely cared what the outcome was. Unfortunately, that had led Allen to establish a pattern of making poor choices.

Joan and Andy had always wanted Allen to be well liked and they had put a great deal of emphasis on that. They had viewed that outcome as more important than the choices he made in regard to his relationships. When Jason, the boy down the block, was labeled as a "geek" by some of the popular kids at school, Allen cut off ties with him even though the boy had been a kind and loyal friend for years. Joan and Andy did not explore the whys of the severed relationship, they merely applauded when Allen was invited to a sleepover given by one of the powerful, popular boys in his class. The loss of a true friend was not as important as the perceived outcome of success in being well liked.

As the changes occurred in Joan and Andy's life, they realized that Allen's behavior did not always reflect the values they now held dear. In order to encourage both Allen and Neal to make good choices, Joan and Andy had to be aware of much more than the outcome.

They decided to employ a tactic advanced in the Understanding Your Teenager Seminar—to "catch your child in the act of doing something good." After all, that's what they had done when they encouraged Neal after he congratulated the other football player. Now they were on the alert to catch Allen "in the act."

It didn't take long to find an opening. One day Jason, apparently of hardy enough character to disregard Allen's cold shoulder, called to see if Allen wanted to ride bikes. Joan knew by the interested look in his eye that Allen wanted to take his old friend up on the offer.

"Mom," he yelled with one hand covering the mouthpiece of the phone, "Can I go bike riding with Jason? He just got a new ten-speed and he really wants me to see it. Can I go?"

"Sure," Joan replied. "Just be back by six for dinner."

As Allen ran past his mom to get his bike and get going, Joan commented. "I heard you talking to Jason about his bike. It really sounds like a neat one. I know he enjoyed telling you about it. Have fun!"

Joan encouraged Allen's good choice to extend kindness and to express interest in another person.

Joan and Andy will have to be conscious of the potential mistake of *demanding* good choices from their sons at the ages of ten and fourteen. They cannot demand that Neal applaud another receiver who scores. They cannot demand that Allen show interest and kindness to a boy in the neighborhood. Oh, they *could* demand it. Just like the father who demanded his nineteen-year-old son go to bed by ten o'clock because of a big test the next day. Probably Neal, Allen, and the adult son would do what was asked, but they will not be encouraged to make that good choice again. They will respond to the demand but not be empowered to choose wisely at the next opportunity. We want to empower our kids by encouraging good choices.

The key to parenting well is to empower your kids, and you do this by complimenting them for the things they do well. When they come up with a good insight or make a good decision, that is the moment to compliment them for their good thinking and capable actions.[8]

Undoing habit patterns and rewriting previously accepted scripts will not be easy for Joan and Andy. It will take time and a commitment to encourage their kids to make good choices.

Unless former patterns are destructive (to the boys themselves or to others) it would be best for Joan and Andy to employ the Encouragement guideline when they spot a good choice rather than attempting to continually discourage poor choices. God's Word does not say "Therefore *discourage* one another and tear each other down."

Joan and Andy are now regular attendees at the church at the corner of the park near their home. So are their boys. Both boys are old enough for youth group—Neal in the senior group and Allen in the junior group. Joan and Andy can encourage the boys to participate in these programs. (A good choice.) They can make participation an easy thing by providing transportation to and from the events. Since the youth groups meet on Wednesday evening at 6:30, Joan and Andy can tell the boys that if they want to go to church on those nights, they will do their dishwashing assignments. By doing this, Joan and Andy are encouraging their sons' involvement in something good from both a spiritual and social standpoint.

Encouraging your children to develop friendships with other kids who have high standards of behavior is always a good choice. The young man who exhibited a filthy mouth at the football game is not a good choice for a friend. Parents encouraging their kids to make good choices would not nominate this boy for "peer of the year."

Friendships are important. And peer pressure is a very real thing. It can influence language, behavior, habits, appearance, and on and on. Even adults experience it and it is definitely a factor when you are ten and fourteen like Allen and Neal. Peers do exert pressure, but children choose their peers. They choose which kind of pressure they will experience. If Joan and Andy can help their kids feel good about themselves they are less likely to choose peers with destructive behavior.

As Neal and Allen make good choices about their health and their intellectual growth, these can also be encouraged. Joan and Andy will do well to look for the good choices and applaud them. This encouragement will build the foundation that can help their kids make good choices.

Ruth and James

Finally we turn to Ruth and James. Can they encourage their kids to make good choices? Of course they can. The dynamics of their situation are different, but this guideline can still be effective.

Just as with our other two couples, they will want to focus on the making of good choices rather than the specific outcome that occurs from the choice. That will be easier to do with Christopher, their son who is still at home. Ideas for encouraging Christopher to make good choices would be very similar to the ones given to Joan and Andy. With Marci in college, Ruth and James will have only a few opportunities to witness her choices in action and hence to encourage the good choices. Her life is now much more separate from her parents.

That separation will be the greatest challenge to Ruth and James as they encourage Marci to make good choices. The physical separation of Marci at college and her parents at home represents other separations as well. As a college student, Marci is transitioning into adulthood. Actually, she is finishing the transition which began with adolescence. Marci is now physically separated from her parents and is also separated socially and emotionally. Her dependence on her parents, while not totally absent, is markedly decreased from even the year before when she was a senior in high school.

Our second son went to college this year. I wrote about this phenomenon for a fall issue of the *Hearts at Home* magazine: "Now I no longer play a starring role in his life. At best I am a supporting actress." As parents, we must learn to let go. And with that letting go, comes a change in our interaction with our child, even in the area of encouragement.

Just as we noted earlier, the beginning stages of encouragement could actually be a time of demanding good choices. Then a transition is made to parental encouragement. And finally, we move from the encouragement a parent exhibits to the encouragement given by a friend.

Even though Ruth and James are, have been, and will always be Marci's parents, her need for "parenting" will typically diminish as time passes. Her need for love and friendship, however, will not diminish. In order to maintain an active, positive, encouraging relationship with Marci, Ruth and James will have to make the transition to fill her changing needs.

As they seek to encourage Marci to make good choices, they must attempt to encourage her as adult to adult, not as adult to child. For example, rather than demand or even suggest that Marci make the good choice to attend church on campus (or to wait until they learn that this positive scenario has occurred),

Ruth and James can encourage the good choice as they might encourage an adult friend. Ruth and James can plan a trip to visit Marci on Sunday and include church on campus as part of their agenda. Then they simply invite Marci to church and dinner as they would invite and encourage a friend.

Ruth, who is the parent feeling the most intense desire to help their kids make good choices, will have to be very aware of Marci's leap in the direction of adulthood. It is possible, in her desire to make a positive (though tardy) decision to encourage Marci to make good choices, that she might inadvertently fail to give Marci the freedom she desires or even demands. Ruth must not let her longing to interact with Marci and encourage her become a negative situation. It is important for Ruth to be available to Marci, but not to be smothering.

How can Ruth enhance and encourage their relationship with Marci away at school? One suggestion is to make calling home very easy. Ruth could give Marci a phone card or even obtain a toll-free phone number for their home. And then, when those calls come from Marci (not on demand, of course), Ruth will want to be available and encouraging but not demanding or needy. She will want to interact with Marci as she would interact and encourage another adult.

God's Word tells us that "A friend loves at all times" (Proverbs 17:17a). Being a friend and interacting at an adult level means attempting to share that agape love with another person. "He who covers over an offense promotes love, but whoever repeats the matter separates close friends" (Proverbs 17:9). That is another good parameter for adult encouragement.

Because Ruth desires to encourage Marci to make good choices, she will have to look on that task as she would the task of encouraging a friend to make good choices. That is not to say that Ruth and James are not still responsible as parents to step in and discourage dangerous or intentionally or irresponsibly wrong choices. At this stage, that is still their parental duty. Ideally the modeling and encouragement given through the prior years will make these potential interventions very uncommon.

Encouraging the making of good choices is important at every stage of parenting. It is the next layer of the solid foundation that will help your kids make good choices.

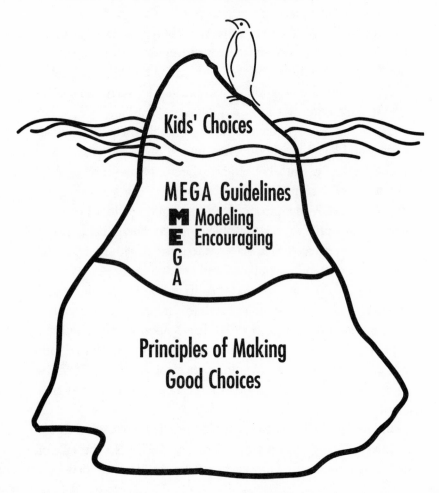

Kids' Choices

MEGA Guidelines
M Modeling
E Encouraging
G
A

Principles of Making
Good Choices

EIGHT

Choosing to Guide Good Choices

Talk about them when you sit at home and when you walk
along the road, when you lie down and when you get up.

DEUTERONOMY 6:7b

The next MEGA guideline we want to examine is G—guiding your kids to good choices. Guiding is different from encouraging. It is more hands-on, more direct. Just as a guide takes you on an adventure, we can guide our kids on the adventure of making good choices. Many times guidance is synonymous with the wise counsel sought in good decision making.

Our kids will obtain guidance from many different sources as they go through their growing-up years. As parents, you will be a major source of guidance but you will not be the sole source. In the last chapter, we talked about encouraging our kids to select peers that will have a positive influence on them. "A righteous man is cautious in friendship, but the way of the wicked leads them astray" (Proverbs 12:26). Peers definitely influence one another. They are one source of guidance.

Additionally, kids are influenced and receive guidance from other adults besides their parents. Teachers, especially in a self-contained elementary classroom, spend close to eight hours a day with their students and can provide guidance in many areas beyond academics. So can Sunday school teachers.

Kids are also guided by the media. These forces and others

can influence or guide our kids. Before we examine our three families and take a look at how each of those parents can guide good choices, let's evaluate these other forms of counsel and see how they can be a source of wise guidance. When children ask someone other than their parents for counsel, how can we increase the possibility that the counsel they receive is wise?

God's Word Is Our Guide

First and foremost, the more our children know what is said in God's Word, the more accurately they will be able to judge whether counsel is wise or unwise. "I will instruct you and teach you in the way you should go; I will counsel you and watch over you" (Psalm 32:8).

I had an interesting conversation one evening with a young girl who was just preparing to turn sixteen. As we sat beside one another on the top bleacher before a high school basketball game, she began to chat with me about a book she was reading.

"It's really good," she explained. "It's a love story."

"I'm reading a mystery right now," I replied. "Tell me about your book."

"Well," she began, "the main character is a high school girl who has vowed to remain a virgin until marriage." ["Good," I thought.] "But she meets the most wonderful guy and she is sure that she's going to marry him someday. He thinks they'll marry too! Anyway," she continued matter-of-factly, "she decides to sleep with him and lose her virginity. And she is really glad she did."

I learned long ago not to react when high school kids tell me things like that. You know, no "surprise in the eyes," no gasp, or sigh of disappointment. Instead I've learned to internalize my displeasure, frustration, or mortification so that the conversation can continue.

"Hmmm," I said unemotionally, "so now what's happening in the story?"

"Well," my young friend continued undaunted, "it was the most wonderful experience she had ever had and now she is *sure* that they will marry and have a wonderful life together."

"Did you know that, statistically speaking, the odds are against that marriage, one, ever occurring, or two, being a success if it does happen?" I asked. "Even if they get married, the fact that they had sex outside of marriage goes against their chance for a lasting marriage."

"Really?" she said, totally amazed. "Why is that, I wonder?"

"I think that it's because the girl and guy in the story are breaking one of God's rules. God says to abstain from fornication. That's sex outside of marriage," I added, thinking of the King James Version of 1 Thessalonians 4:3.

"Why does he care?" she blurted out. "It seems to me he makes a bunch of rules to keep people from having fun!"

At that point I told this young lady a story. It was a tale of something that had happened in our home on Christmas years before, and I hoped it would illustrate the answer to her question.

One year when our kids were little, they got a game for Christmas. It was a "Clue" game and it had appeared on the Christmas list of both of the older boys. When they opened the game, the last present under the tree (To: Matthew, Aaron, and Jonathan From: Mom and Dad), they wanted to play it immediately.

That was fine with me. And so I started to read the rules on the top of the box.

"Stop reading the rules, Mom," the older boys said almost in unison. "We know how to play this game. We've played it at Luke's house before. Come on, Mom. We want to start playing."

So I acquiesced, put the box lid over to the side, and the game began. After just a few minutes, it was pretty obvious that they did not really know the rules of the game. The fact that no one knew the rules soon led to an argument between the boys.

"You can't move into that room yet!"

"Yes I can! You have the rules mixed up!"

The arguing intensified and ultimately no one wanted to play the game. Every single player was unhappy and disappointed and we definitely had no winner.

As I finished telling this story, I drew an analogy.

"God's Word is like the rules on the top of the box. He gives us those rules so that we know how to play the game of life. Without the rules, playing the game is frustrating and we never know how to win.

"God doesn't give us rules like 'abstain from fornication' to take away our fun," I told her. "He gives us those rules to make our lives *more* fun and more productive—to make us winners. His Word is 'the rules on the top of the box.'"

My young friend understood what I had said. I hope the analogy helped her see the very positive aspect of God's Word being our guide. Teaching our kids God's Word and its relevance, and teaching them about God's loving nature will help them to be able to use the Bible as a guide. It will also help them as they evaluate the guidance of others. "Listen to advice and accept instruction, and in the end you will be wise" (Proverbs 19:20).

The Media's Influence

What about the guidance of the media? Most parents would be quick to say that the media is one source of guidance they hope their kids choose to ignore. Undoubtedly, the media can have an incredibly negative influence on children. What do we do as parents? Do we forbid all negative media from entering into our homes? Do we "unplug" when the children arrive on the scene and only "plug in" again after they are adults? That is one option (be it ever so drastic), but it is probably not the most effective one for guiding our kids to make good choices. By eliminating all negative media (almost an impossibility in our culture) we are eliminating the need for our kids to make choices—at least to make choices when they are with us or in our homes.

Can you control the billboard on the interstate highway with the scantily clad model? What about the nightly news with scathing reports of impropriety? Or the television commercial in the midst of an acceptable show which sells its product by giving a sexual message? Because the negative guidance is so subtle and permeates almost every aspect of our society, we must do more than merely control it. We must teach our children to be discerning.

The media will definitely attempt to influence our kids (and adults too, for that matter). We can control certain aspects of it. First of all, the television and VCR are not child-care providers. They are classified as entertainment. If children are indiscriminately allowed to watch TV or videos, we are allowing these media sources to mold our kids. We, as parents, must choose what is appropriate and what is inappropriate for the age of our children. When an inappropriate interruption (in other words, a commercial) appears during our appropriate selection, it provides a teachable moment. We, as parents, can comment on the advertisement and talk about it with our kids. Many times that is better than simply turning the channel. It gives us the opportunity to educate our children on what is inappropriate and why.

We are sports fans at our home. You would think that there would be very little questionable programming during a professional football game. Wishful thinking. Occasionally the camera pans to the cheerleaders. Unfortunately, those poor girls are underdressed. (You'd think they could afford an entire uniform.) When the camera focuses on the over-endowed, undergarmented young women, my boys hear me say (time and time again), "Those girls need a turtleneck."

When a movie we are watching lets an undesirable (and usually unnecessary) word slip into the script, I say, "Grandma Ruthie always said that using words like that was a sign of a poor vocabulary."

When one TV character refers to another in derogatory terms, I say, "That was rude!"

When two people hop into bed with one another, I inquire, "Did they get married during the commercial?"

These words of mine were and are as predictable as the inappropriate words or behaviors the media is likely to present. In fact, my boys have told me that even when I am nowhere to be found, the messages I have said for years still play in their heads. Good. The guidance continues.

It is important to teach our kids to be discerning about the media, to realize when dialogue is rude or inappropriate or sacrilegious. Ultimately we parents won't be there to change the channel. Our kids must learn when that maneuver is necessary. They must evaluate if and when the media is giving wise counsel and guiding them to make a good choice.

Other Adults

What about the guidance of adults other than parents? It is important for our kids to have positive adult role models, encouragers, and guidance-givers in their lives in addition to their parents. These adults can act to reinforce the values and principles taught at home. Contrarily, it is possible that adults will choose to reinforce bad choices. How can we help our kids be discerning about guidance from other adults?

There was a song popular several years ago. The chorus went like this: "Who to, and not to, listen to?" And the entire song was dedicated to helping teenagers be discriminating about whom to seek counseling and guidance from. How can our kids tell whom to listen to?

As a youth leader for nearly two decades, I have taught a lesson on precisely that question numerous times. I tell teenagers to imagine that they have a big filing cabinet in their heads and that everyone they have ever come into contact with has a paper in the file drawer.

When we first meet someone, the paper that we file will probably be blank. Then, as we interact with that person, we will be able to make observations about the person's behavior. Again, God's Word will be our measuring stick.

Because we know that no one is perfect except Jesus, the paper in our file for each acquaintance will not stay perfect. Our observations will reveal poor choices and decisions made which are contrary to God's Word. When those occur, we simply poke a little hole in the paper.

When we realize that a person has chosen to lie, we poke a hole in their paper file. When we observe them cheating another tiny hole is poked. They gossip about someone and we poke another hole. This is how the file system works. Only the paper for Jesus remains completely intact.

Now, if we have a file on someone who is notorious, whose life choices are consistently in contrast to the ones God gives us, his paper would be filled with holes. If his offenses were repeated again and again, the tiny holes would eventually run together and form even larger ones.

Now that you have a clear picture of the filing system, those papers can really come in handy. Many times people can *say* all the right things ... at least it seems like they are saying the right things. They offer guidance and it *seems* to be legitimate and in your best interests. But how do you know whom to listen to? Simple.

At this point I bring out a cup of sugar. The sugar represents the words we are hearing. Those words seem to be sweet just like the sugar. Maybe we *should* take the guidance this person is offering. There is a simple test that can be done to see "Who to, and not to, listen to."

All you need to do is to pull that person's paper from your file and pour his talk (the sugar) on to the paper. Now sift the talk (the sugar) through the walk (the paper). If there are great big holes in the walk, discrepancies you have observed between this person's behavior and the Word of God, most of the sugar will fall straight through. If the paper has only tiny pin pricks, most of the talk will stay put. Sift the talk through the walk.

"God told me that you should _____ (fill in the blank)." Sift the talk through the walk before you take the guidance.

"You need to _____ (fill in the blank)." Sift the talk through the walk before you take the guidance.

"I think you should _____ (fill in the blank)." Sift the talk through the walk before you take the guidance.

If we teach our kids to think this way, we may be able to spare them the pain of listening to unwise counsel and poor guidance.

Peers

Peers provide guidance also, sometimes good and sometimes poor. Always remember that peers are selected. Model good peer preference and encourage your kids to select peers who consistently make good choices. Those peers are more likely to choose to guide others to make good choices too.

I remember standing in my kitchen one evening, washing dishes after my two older sons and several of their friends finished up a snack of chili, crackers, and cheese. (Snacks for sixteen-year-old boys constitute full meals for most of us.) As I washed the big pot, one of the friends, John, made a very pleasant observation.

"Gee, Kendra," John said glancing around at the half dozen or so boys in the kitchen, "we're *all* designated drivers!"

To him, that was just a slice of interesting trivia. To me it was a tremendous blessing. All of those boys—John, Bryan, Brian, Mike, Matthew, Aaron, and Nathan—had made the good choice not to drink. And that was the peer pressure applied in that group. That was the guidance they gave to one another. We can encourage our kids to choose peers who will provide guidance to make good choices. We can help our kids have confidence to avoid poor guidance.

All of those influences—peers, the media, and other adults can give either good or poor guidance to our kids. We can help our children learn to discern when it comes to that guidance.

And now, the biggest influence: the guide who has the most clout—the parents. Let's take a look at our three sets of parents as they employ this aspect of the MEGA guidelines to make their children's foundation even more secure. Let's see how they can guide good choices.

Lisa and Brian

Lisa and Brian are in the wonderful position of knowing, before their child even arrives, that they can choose to guide his good choices. In the adventure of life, Lisa and Brian have decided to be intentional in their influence of their child.

"My son, keep your father's commands and do not forsake your mother's teaching. Bind them upon your heart forever; fasten them around your neck. When you walk, they will guide you; when you sleep, they will watch over you; when you awake, they will speak to you" (Proverbs 6:20-23).

Our commands and teaching as parents have the power to guide, watch over, and speak to our children.

My Parents Taught Me

Last week at senior high youth, we were discussing relation-ships—relationships with God, parents, and friends. At one point I asked the kids to share one thing that their parents had taught them. The answers were varied and thoughtful.

"My parents taught me how to speak with adults."

"Mine taught me not to always follow the crowd."

"My dad taught me how to work hard."

They were not at a loss to think of things their parents had taught them. Those things were a few of the guiding principles in their lives.

Lisa and Brian will be able to teach their child God's Word, his nature, and to "love the Lord your God with all your heart and with all your soul and with all your mind" (Matthew 22:37). They will be able to guide their child to see God at work in everyday things.

Teachable Moments

One evening I sat between two kindergarteners at a football game. They were full of pep and had lots of things to tell me.

"Look at my finger, Kendra," one said directing my attention to his extended pinkie. "I cut it last week."

Not to be outdone, the child on my left quickly interjected, "Look here! I had a bad scrape on my hand from falling on the sidewalk!"

I looked first at the pinkie and then the hand and, to the naked eye, both appeared 100 percent healthy.

"Those look pretty good now," I said. "God must have healed them up!"

"God?" one boy said incredulously, wondering what in the world God had to do with the whole thing. "What do you mean? Is he magic or something?"

Obviously, no one had ever told him about the miraculous power of God.

"No," I countered. "He's not magic. He made your body so that it could heal up from a cut or a scrape. Isn't that neat?"

A teachable moment. Lisa and Brian will have many teachable moments when they can help their child identify the awesome power of God. A child can be guided to recognize God in the big and little things.

Lisa and Brian can guide their child in his interaction with others. I remember my husband teaching our children to ask themselves the question "What is my goal?" *before* reacting to a situation. This question which they employed is very similar to the question "What would Jesus do?" that became popular with kids and adults alike. It is a wonderful guiding principle. "WWJD?" "What is my goal?" The answer to those questions can serve your children well in their interaction with others.

"A wise man's heart guides his mouth, and his lips promote instruction" (Proverbs 16:23).

Just as a guide on an adventure points out the pitfalls and pluses of the trip, that will be Lisa and Brian's task. Their discipline will establish guidance for behavior.

"Discipline your son, and he will give you peace; he will bring delight to your soul" (Proverbs 29:17).

"He who spares the rod hates his son, but he who loves him is careful to discipline him" (Proverbs 13:24).

In this day of readily identified abuse or suspected abuse, we might tend to forgo discipline as a guide, but that is a mistake.

"Healthy families apply healthy boundaries."[9] Boundaries are an important part of guidance. These boundaries themselves and the motivation for establishing them must, of course, be appropriate.

Who's in Charge?

Recently I spoke to a group of young mothers. After the message, I had many moms congregate to visit with me or to ask specific questions. My message that day dealt with the relationship of husband and wife. One mom stayed to the back of the line, waiting until most of the others had gone on to the refreshment table. Finally she approached.

"My husband and I are having some difficulties in our marriage right now," she began. "We have one son who is two and a half and after your talk today, I'm beginning to think that maybe the way I am treating my son is part of the reason we're having marital problems."

"What do you mean?" I inquired.

"Well, I just love my son so much that I let him dictate a lot of what happens in our home. For example, if we have plans to go out and my son wants us to stay home," she said, "we change our plans."

The thought of a two-and-a-half-year-old being in charge of the adults in his home left me a little breathless.

"Your son needs you to set the guidelines for him," I said. "At two and a half years old he is not capable of being in charge. In fact, you are doing him a disservice by allowing it," I told the mother. She undoubtedly loved him. But as parents, we show that love in many ways, including setting boundaries, administering discipline and in general, being the parent—the one in charge, guiding our children's choices.

After a few more minutes of conversation, the mom was sure that indeed she had inappropriately given up the parenting-guiding role in this circumstance. She resolved to begin immediately to express her love for her son (and her husband) by setting boundaries for their child.

What? No Mothers?

One day I was listening to the radio as I cooked. The program playing was a call-in show, a question and answer format dealing with moral issues. The host was Dr. Laura Schlessinger. Although she can be somewhat terse and abrasive, I enjoy hearing her common sense, Old Testament answers to the questions she receives.

My sons do not typically listen to Dr. Laura's program. In fact, when they do, they usually find it rather annoying and even a little ridiculous. Their biggest contention is with the callers. The dilemmas, in their opinion, are for the most part, very elementary to solve.

When my eldest son entered the kitchen that afternoon and heard the show that was on the radio, he asked quite simply, "Don't those people calling in have mothers?"

What a fine compliment to motherhood! In his opinion, only a person without a mother (or father) would have to call a radio talk show and ask for help on a moral issue. If they had parents, they would already know the answer, for their parents would have provided guidance for them.

You're the Expert

When Lisa and Brian's child is young, his parents will have the overwhelming percentage of influence on his life. And, they will be, in their child's opinion, the experts on every issue.

Ever since my kids were young, I have jotted down stories and interesting things that they said. My journal noted that in 1986, when Aaron was only four, he asked me when "God was coming back?" I also recorded my simple answer to his question.

"The Bible says that no one knows the time or place."

Aaron's reaction to my answer was precious. "Not even *you?*"

As I look at my eighteen- (soon to be nineteen-) year-old son today, it's hard to believe that he innocently and genuinely believed that I knew *everything*. Somewhere along the line, that changed. He discovered the truth.

Lisa and Brian's child will also be certain that they, indeed, are all-knowing. And just like Aaron, that will change. In fact, as the years pass, it is possible that, for a brief period of time, Lisa and Brian will not only leave the status of all-knowing, but may actually temporarily enter the no-knowing status. Guidance is still possible, necessary, and a parent's responsibility even in those years ... the years that Joan and Andy's boys are in at the moment.

Joan and Andy

Joan and Andy's sons, Neal and Allen, were fourteen and ten when their parents made a major change in their lives. It was then that Joan and Andy accepted Christ and began the journey of the Christian life. Becoming Christians changed many things in their lives and household. For the first time ever, Joan and Andy had a genuine desire to model, encourage, and guide Neal and Allen to make good choices. Because this was a *new* attitude, it was not as simple for them as it will be for Lisa and Brian. For all their children's lives up to this point, Neal and Allen's parents have been guiding them (intentionally or inadvertently) down one path; *now* they desire to divert from that path and move in another direction. As they initiate this change toward godly choices, Joan and Andy will have to be very patient.

Joan and Andy need to realize the dilemma they have created by guiding their kids down the wrong path for so many years. That first path, the one leading away from Christ, is the more familiar and more comfortable. For all their lives, Joan and Andy have modeled and encouraged this path and the boys have been guided to travel it with their parents.

The old path included Sunday morning snoozing. The new path includes a trip to Sunday school and worship instead. The old path included self-serving behavior (for instance, lying if it advanced the cause). The new path discourages lying and deceit. It used to be OK to cheat and to use people if the desired end was achieved. Now that is deemed inappropriate. Why?

As Joan and Andy guide their kids to change paths and to make good choices, they will have to be prepared to constantly answer the question "Why?" Joan and Andy must be able to explain the desired changes in their home, their lifestyles, their behavior, their focus. And these explanations will have to be legitimate. No, "because I said so, that's why." Their children will be searching for reasonable explanations. Joan and Andy will need to be able to justify the changes that are being made. Neal and Allen are old enough to understand and they will want to know *why* their family is not staying on its original path.

Joan and Andy will likely have the opportunity in their explanations to admit their mistaken choice to travel the first path and they can apologize for their previously improper guidance. Then they will need to be patient. And Joan and Andy will need to be true to the new path and stay away from their old patterns of behavior. Their children will be watching.

Neal and Allen will also be watching their father, specifically, to see if his new beliefs will negatively affect his manliness. Their dad was a man's man. Will Christianity make him effeminate?

The answer, of course, is no. It is likely to change behavior the boys may have typically classified as masculine (behavior like drinking or using inappropriate language). It will be up to Andy to patiently guide the boys to see the true picture of masculinity. The man who has self-control is much more mature and masculine than the one who heads into an argument with both fists swinging. If Neal and Allen have the wrong sense of masculinity and the wrong identifiers, Andy will have the task of guiding them into the truth. His commitment to godly behavior and to leadership of his family will help to facilitate this guidance. Andy will need to be active in his role as a parent.

It is possible that the boys, especially Neal, the older child, may have developed unhealthy alliances which could give him negative guidance. Since the household standards for peers only recently became an issue, some of Neal's previously selected friends may now fall into the unacceptable column. It is also possible that after the change in his parents' lives they found that some of their own peers fell into that column too. This is another area for conversation, guidance, and modeling. Joan and Andy will have to make changes in their peer group in order to support their life changes. Neal and Allen can be encouraged to do likewise. Again, patience is an important aspect. The children can be guided in their evaluation of current and potential friends. They can be encouraged to make friends in youth group and church who are more likely to advocate the choices Joan and Andy desire for their children. Joan and Andy can also include the boys' former friends in the new activities in their lives now with the hopes that they will be positively influenced.

As Neal and Allen observe their parents modeling the making of good choices and the decision-making process consistently, and witness them encouraging good choices, they will be more willing to allow their parents to guide them into good choices. All of the MEGA guidelines go hand in hand.

Ruth and James

Our final family, Ruth and James and their kids Marci and Christopher, have an additional factor to deal with when it comes to guidance. On a very positive note, Christopher has already been in the habit of seeking guidance from some very positive sources: his grandmother, his church, and his youth leaders. In his case, Ruth and James merely need to guide him to do more of the same.

With Marci already at college, direct opportunities for

guidance in her life are definitely limited. The most obvious opportunities will occur if and when Marci asks for guidance. There will be numerous decisions she must make that are new to her as a college freshman. If she feels that her parents are interested and somewhat knowledgeable, she may choose to ask for their counsel.

"Should I drop political science? I'm behind in my reading and I can take it next semester when my other class work is lighter."

"I'm thinking about upgrading my computer. My old one is really slow and I think I can trade it in and get a new one for under $2000. What do you think?"

"My roommate situation isn't working out. Sheila is very moody and wants her boyfriend in our room all the time. Should I move out next semester?"

When offering guidance to your adult or nearly adult children it is always good to offer it with the same mind-set you would have for a friend. When Gloria asks me for guidance or counsel in some area, I do not assume that my suggestion will automatically be taken. Instead, I offer guidance to the best of my ability. If God's Word applies, I include that in my guidance. There are no strings attached to my guidance. That posture is most appropriate with adult children too. My advice or counsel is not the law and I need to assure the person seeking guidance that my feelings will not be hurt if, in the final analysis, my guidance is rejected. That is our role when we guide our adult children. "The Bible doesn't talk about adult children obeying parents. In Ephesians 6:1, the original Greek word refers to young children, not those who are fully grown."[10]

The other possibility that Ruth and James have for guidance of Marci is to share situations they are personally experiencing— guidance they are receiving from God's Word and from other godly sources. It is important to simply offer these experiences as potential learning moments with no other ulterior motives or hidden agendas. By sharing our personal experiences with God's guidance and by offering other nuggets of guidance, we are adding to the foundation. Guiding good choices is a very important part of helping our kids make good choices.

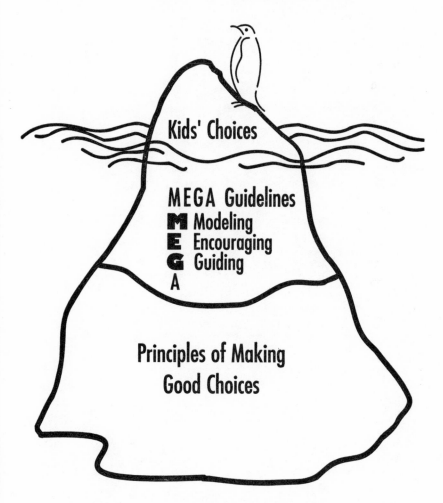

NINE

Choosing to Allow Choices

Choose you this day whom ye will serve.

JOSHUA 24:15a, KJV

We are ready to examine the last of the MEGA guidelines for parents—allowing our children to make choices. You may notice that the word "good" is not found proceeding the word "choices" in this guideline as it was in all the others. We must allow our children to make choices, both good and bad, and to take responsibility for those choices.

When our eldest son was eleven years old, he received a birthday gift of twenty dollars from my mother. This was a lot of money and he was determined to spend it on something very special. Not too many days after he received it, we took off together for the toy store. I wish that I had checked my watch when we entered and exited the store, because I know I run the risk of being charged with exaggeration since I have no cold hard facts or records. Being very sensitive to that, however, my estimate is that we spent over twenty-five minutes in the toy store looking for the perfect selection. He had decided to buy a computer game and he diligently read the back of every game that he had deemed a candidate for purchase. Finally, after the analysis was complete, Matthew made his choice. We marched to the checkout counter and took our place in line. As we waited, all the "impulse" items on the counter sparkled, chimed, and begged for Matthew's attention. Sure enough, he began to quickly examine them and as our turn for checkout arrived and the clerk asked if she could help us, Matthew surprisingly changed his mind and exchanged the well-researched game for an item on the counter.

"Are you sure?" I asked, trying to encourage him to rethink his decision.

"Yes," he said. "This is what I want."

So he purchased the impulse item and our shopping trip was complete. As he headed for the car, he was already engrossed in his new gadget. He had extracted it from the package and was beginning to play with it as we settled into the car.

I'm not sure what this handheld game was *supposed* to do. He hadn't taken the time to show me its attributes and challenges before he bought it. Regardless of what it was *supposed* to do, it must not have done it, for before we were out of the parking lot of the Tippecanoe Mall in Lafayette, Indiana, Matthew had reached across the seat and handed me the toy.

"Here, Mom," he said despondently. "Take this. It's just junk and it makes me feel bad!"

I took the rejected toy in my hand and everything within me wanted to cry out, "Here's another twenty dollars. Go back into the store and get the first toy you chose."

I wanted to fix my son's poor choice. But, through the grace of God, I did not do it! In reality, I probably did not have an extra twenty dollars to give him to spend. Praise God!

Instead I simply said, "That's alright, Matthew, Grandma will probably give you another twenty dollars next year."

What did he learn from that depressing trip to the toy store? Well, obviously, he learned that you can only spend money one time. He had made a poor choice on the spending of that money and now it was gone. That is an important life lesson for our day and age. Too many children (and adults too) are spending money even after it is gone and are experiencing financial crises in their lives.

Many years later that same son got his first "real job" for the summer. It dawned on him a few days before work started that he would need a little different wardrobe than he had. Jeans would not suffice for this job in the office of the local CPA.

So one bright and beautiful summer day he headed for the shopping mall with my credit card, to make some purchases. After an hour or so, the reality (and potential horror) of the situation hit me. I had just sent a seventeen-year-old boy to the mall with my credit card, very few instructions, and no spending limit. Yikes! I must have been experiencing temporary insanity. Oh well, there was nothing I could do now but wait for his return.

An hour or so later, in he walked. He carried two or three very large sacks and proudly plopped them in front of me in preparation for the fashion show. As he held up a pair of trousers from the first sack, his words brought a smile to my lips.

"These pants," he began, "are only one size too big. And they were five dollars. I can wear a belt."

By the time he was done displaying every item, I realized that he had spent only about sixty dollars and he had greatly increased his wardrobe. Good choices!

I will probably always believe that his poor choice to throw away twenty dollars on the impulse birthday gift so long ago contributed to his good choices years later. I realize that it was not the sole contributor, but the life lesson couldn't have hurt.

Mom, I Forgot My ...

One afternoon I found myself visiting with a woman, a mother, whom I only knew casually. (When you are a "visiting" type of person, these circumstances don't really surprise you.) Anyway, as we stood and chatted, she mentioned the fact that she had delivered her son's lunch to him at school all five days in the past week. In other words, there was not one day, Monday through Friday, when her son remembered to take his lunch with him.

I found that fact more than a little alarming. There are certainly times when I have made a quick trip to school with a forgotten trumpet or a permission slip left on the refrigerator, but I still found the thought of a child forgetting the same thing, his lunch, five days in a row, excessively irresponsible.

There are a few more facts that contributed to my alarm. This young man's mother works outside the home. Their home is about five miles east of school and she works about five miles west of school. According to my calculations, that meant that she had to travel another twenty miles each day in order to deliver the forgotten lunch. That's one hundred miles for the week! And to give you an even more complete picture, the forgetful son was not five, he was fifteen years old!

As she told me of her tiresome week delivering forgotten lunches, it was all I could do not to scream, "What was a fifteen-year-old boy doing asking his mom to bring him his sack lunch five days in a row?"

When I gently asked why he didn't eat the hot lunch at school, she was quick to explain, "He doesn't like school lunches."

At that moment, I felt a tremendous wave of thankfulness

because I did not have a daughter who might someday fall in love with this "no school lunch" kid and marry him. Can you imagine the dilemma that young lady would find herself in?

That mother, driven no doubt by a stilted view of love, was creating a monster—a young man who was not allowed to choose poorly and suffer the consequences. How sad!

We do our children a tremendous disservice when we protect them from making choices or fail to allow them to experience the good or bad consequences of their choices. One of the emotions a parent must evict in order to make the good choice to allow their kids to choose is the desire to "fix" everything. That is not reality and that is not a measure of love for a child. Please understand, I am not talking about being an advocate for your child when that is necessary. I am talking about allowing kids to make and enjoy reasonable choices. Allowing choices to be made is the fourth of the MEGA guidelines for parents.

Lisa and Brian

Once again Lisa and Brian are starting with a perfect record— no mistakes when it comes to allowing their child to choose. From the very beginning they will be able to allow their child to make choices appropriate to his age and maturity level. As stated before, an infant does not have the intellectual capacity to make choices. As that child grows and matures, the ability to make choices, the desire to make choices, and the necessity of allowing choices will grow and develop too. In regard to Lisa and Brian and their unborn child, their family of the future, we are going to examine two distinct areas of allowing kids to choose.

The first area is in regard to general choices, good and bad, that will come his way. Can Lisa and Brian allow choices, good and bad, in order to train their child in the art of making good choices? How can they determine what choices to allow?

Picture, if you will, a young child in a playpen playing happily. That playpen restricts the child's access and protects him from potential harm. He cannot reach the iron on the ironing board or the electrical outlet. He cannot touch the stove or climb on or fall from the shelves. He is restricted and protected. (And in some instances, things are protected from him too.)

The picture of a young child in a playpen can give us a picture of parenting. We may or may not choose to employ an actual playpen, but our parenting, like a playpen, employs both restriction and protection. We do not allow young children an abundance of freedom in making choices. We restrict their choices and protect them.

As that young child grows and matures, his world of choices grows too. The child now no longer has the restriction and protection of a playpen, but has the full access of the fenced-in yard. He has more choices he can make. He has access to more things and to more adventures, and hopefully his parents have helped him develop more fully his ability to make good choices. The fence around the backyard still acts to restrict and protect the youngster, but not to the extent of the playpen. There are now more choices allowed.

Before long the child is old enough to play in the neighborhood. There is no literal fence around the neighborhood, but there are distinct boundaries—again restricting and protecting.

The "fences" of life keep expanding as children grow and develop. As their skill of making good choices increases, their sphere of freedom can increase. There is not a set date or time for each promotion. A parent must be in tune to the maturity of their child. It is just as detrimental to leave a child in a playpen past the appropriate time as it is to send him into the world when he is prepared only for the fenced-in yard.

Obviously, Lisa and Brian's goal is to prepare their child for an adulthood with very few "fences." In order to do that, they will have to allow choices (good and poor) along the way at each stage. They will need to allow their child to accept the responsibility for choices made. They will need to be realistic in their look at their child's abilities to make choices and not hamstring him by treating him like a baby when he is well beyond those years or, contrarily, push him into situations for which he lacks maturity.

Interestingly enough, the word picture of our playpen-fence has some scientifically substantiated validity. It has been found that school playgrounds with fences encourage play and activity to the very perimeters. Unfenced, unrestricted, unprotected areas tend to elicit play huddled toward the center of the area, away from the perimeter. Fences, definite boundaries, allow children the restriction and protection they desire.

Square Peg—Round Hole
The other, completely distinct aspect of allowing your kids to make choices, is much more personalized and individualized. We have all heard the saying "You can't put a square peg in a round hole." Trying to do that is a poor choice.

Lisa and Brian's child will be born with certain innate abilities and interests. Obviously, nurture will greatly influence those. It is important, however, not to try to "nurture" that square peg into the round hole. Here is where allowing choices comes in again. Lisa and Brian will need to allow their child to develop his God-given skills and interests. The child who seems to have been born with a ball in his hand—tossing it and kicking it and chasing it—might be innately interested in physical activity. His sibling may be more musical. Perhaps problem solving is the child's bent. Or maybe he is a natural artist.

As parents we can help our children develop in many aspects but it is foolish to demand a child to excel in athletics, for example, when he seemingly has no innate interest or ability. Lisa and Brian will have the opportunity to allow their child to develop his God-given talents and abilities. They will have a more satisfied child and a better relationship with him, if they follow his lead and allow their child to set the course for his own interests. Once those are established, Lisa and Brian will be able to help their child to develop those talents to the glory of God.

The challenge of allowing your child to move into his area of innate talent and excel is one that will require a discerning parent. Allowing our children to develop in areas we may not be interested in is sometimes difficult. It is always easier to have a "chip off the old block."

The father who is a fine pianist may not *want* to allow his son to develop his interest and talent in soccer. The mother who was an all-state softball player may have difficulty allowing her daughter's choice to learn ballet. The engineer wants his son to be an engineer. The golfer gives his slightly uncoordinated daughter a set of golf clubs for her thirteenth birthday. The basketball coach requires his son to shoot free throws each evening, like it or not.

You get the picture. This part of allowing choices can be very difficult for some parents. But, if it is not done, future parent-child relationships can be severely damaged.

Lisa and Brian will want to allow their child to develop his God-given talents and abilities. Furthermore, they will want to allow the "fences" of their child's life to expand as they allow him to make ever-expanding choices. Allowing choices is a guideline that contributes to the strong foundation for their child.

A note should probably be inserted at this point about allowing children to choose in areas that are beyond their abilities or responsibilities. I have witnessed incidences when a young child was given a say, perhaps even a vote equal to his parents in a family issue. "Where should we go on vacation this year?" It is fine to solicit the opinions of the family members on issues like these, but undoubtedly a second grader does not understand the financial aspects, for example, of all the various vacation suggestions. If he is allowed to determine the vacation venue, he has been given an adult choice and adult responsibility before he is prepared. Furthermore, his parents have allowed him to have excessive control in the family. This is not what is implied in allowing your kids to make choices.

Joan and Andy

Joan and Andy have a more complicated task when it comes to allowing their kids to make choices. Unlike Lisa and Brian, they did not invest wisely in their children's early years. Now that Joan and Andy desire to help their kids make good choices, their boys, aged ten and fourteen, have moved from the figurative playpen, the fenced-in backyard and the neighborhood restrictions and protection. Now they have boundaries that are much more widespread. Because Joan and Andy failed to monitor the early years of allowing choices with the same fervor they now wish to employ, they will have a more difficult time. Joan and Andy will have to compromise on some issues because of choices they have already allowed their sons to make.

Compromise is a much better tactic than trying to assume the control they previously relinquished. A parent who dogmatically demands control where he has not previously done so may, in fact, gain it. He will not, however, be controlling more than the moment. And furthermore, that parent will be asking for rebellion. Changing the rules, the control, the extent of the choices kids are allowed to make in the "middle of the game" can lead to a great deal of anger.

Neal and Allen have already been allowed to make choices that their parents now deem inappropriate. Unless those are life threatening, it will be best not to begin now to impose restrictions and protection in those areas. You can imagine the difficulty of trying to encourage a toddler to be content in the confinement of a playpen after he has had the freedom of the entire house. Or restricting an older child to the fenced-in yard, not as a punishment or for protection, but to establish this space as his new play area after he has had the freedom of the neighborhood. Those are not productive parenting choices.

For example, one of the choices Neal, Joan and Andy's older son, had always been given was the choice of what music he would listen to. He has had full control over his listening preferences since the very beginning. Now that Joan and Andy have become Christians, they are more aware of the negative qualities of some of the music Neal enjoys.

One obvious option is for them to no longer allow Neal to choose the music he will listen to. (No compromise there.) I'm sure you can see the futility in that possible decision. First of all, control would be limited to only when Neal's parents were able to monitor the music directly. Secondly, by removing a choice Neal had formerly enjoyed, his resentment is almost guaranteed.

Instead of complete control (putting Neal in a "playpen" with all choices of music selection removed) Joan and Andy would do well to compromise. Neal (and Allen too) are old enough to understand that their parents feel that they previously made poor parenting decisions in light of their new belief in Christ. Explaining to their sons *why* they find some of the music offensive is the first step. Then they can make every effort to introduce Neal to Christian music that might have a similar appeal. Perhaps they could request the elimination of one particular group or artist (I use that term loosely) from Neal's collection. If he has invested his own money in the music he possesses, they could offer to buy from Neal some of the CD's that they believe are most detrimental.

It is difficult to regain control and influence, to instill restrictions and protection when they have not previously been there. That is why compromise is important as Joan and Andy allow their kids to make choices.

> Finally, we should allow kids to assert themselves in harmless ways. As we discussed earlier, our teenagers will probably want to act and behave in ways that express their emerging adulthood. As long as the behavior is not harmful or morally wrong, it's generally recommended that we allow it. This strategy may prevent harmful, destructive rebellion later on. Allowing teens to assert themselves in harmless ways reduces their need to rebel.[11]

Joan and Andy will have to allow choices that Lisa and Brian may never face. Unless those choices are too dangerous to allow for error, they will want to allow the choices to be made. Remember that allowing choices is not the only guideline that Joan and Andy are employing. At the same time they are modeling good choices and the decision-making process, encouraging good choices, and guiding good choices. The chances are that the allowing of choices will be positively modified by the boys witnessing all those other guidelines in action.

Ruth and James

Ruth and James will also want to employ the MEGA guideline of allowing choices. There will be no problem allowing their college age daughter, Marci, to make choices. Because she is away from home, it would be difficult, if not impossible, to control her choices. It is also much easier to allow her the responsibility for her choices. In fact, for the most part, Ruth and James will not even know the choices she has made. They will see a reflection of those choices in her grade card and in her peace of mind, but they are not there to monitor each and every choice.

If Marci had chosen to live in her parents' home while attending college or to live at home and work, the "playpen" concept of restriction and protection would still have some application. Each household has rules made to help it function efficiently and happily. If Marci had chosen to remain in her parents' home, those rules would still apply (as they will when she returns home for summer vacations).

Ruth and James may have established the rule of "reporting in" after an evening out. If this is important to them, they do not have to allow Marci to ignore this policy just because she is over eighteen years old. They will probably no longer dictate things like bedtime, but it is certainly not unreasonable to request relative quiet after a certain hour in the evening.

But Marci did not choose to stay at home, so allowing is almost automatic. Is there ever a time when Ruth and James might choose to intervene in allowing Marci to make choices?

Surprisingly, the answer is yes. Again, it is the parents' responsibility to protect their child from potentially dangerous situations. When that child is more adult than child, the "protection" takes a little different form.

Let's say, for example, that Marci chooses to move out of her dorm room and into an apartment with her boyfriend. (This is unlikely in Marci's case because of her commitment to Christ but not outside the realm of possibility.) Assuming that Ruth and James do not approve of this living arrangement, they do not have to condone it. Can they protect Marci from this destructive behavior? Can they forbid her the freedom to make this choice?

Actually, they cannot. But what they *can* do is to discourage it by wise counsel. And they do not have to facilitate it. How would they be facilitating it? If Ruth and James are paying the bills at college and they allow Marci this choice, they are facilitating the choice.

The confrontation is really quite simple.

"Marci, we don't approve of your choice to live with your boyfriend. We cannot stop you from doing this, but we will not contribute to it. If you want to continue in this choice, you will be paying your own bills at college. The choice is yours."

Ruth and James do not have to continue to pay tuition and fees, room and board for Marci. That is not one of the Ten Commandments. They will, however, have to be prepared to do what they say. If they make a statement similar to the one above, and Marci chooses to remain in the immoral lifestyle, they will have to be true to their word and withdraw funding. At all ages, when an ultimatum is given, it must be enforced. That is why it is a wise choice to weigh the pros and cons, seek wise counsel, and evict the emotion before making such an ultimatum.

Years ago a young man was planning a trip to attend a wedding that we had also been invited to attend. The young man called and asked me if he could bring his girlfriend and stay in our home. My answer was certainly. Then he announced to me that they were living together and would want to share a bedroom in our home.

Without excessive emotion (disappointment was the overwhelming one I was experiencing) I told him that would not be possible. I'm sure he already knew my answer. I reassured him that they were welcome in our home, but since they were unmarried, they would be expected to sleep in separate rooms. I added that if this was a problem, there were motels in the area. I did not have to facilitate his poor choice.

As parents of almost adults like Marci, Ruth and James will not be able to exert much control even in potentially dangerous choices. The boundaries of life for restriction and protection are, at this point in parenting, almost nonexistent. There is no longer a playpen or a fenced-in yard or a neighborhood or a community delineating the boundaries. At this stage, the hope is that Marci has developed in her maturity to function with virtually no imposed boundaries other than morality and the law. If she fails to do this well, Ruth and James will have little control. They are not, however, required to facilitate or fund those bad choices. That would, in fact, be a compromise of their values and beliefs.

What about Christopher, their sixteen-year-old son? He is like his sister, Marci, in that he has a track record of good choices. He has had very positive influence from his grandmother and from his involvement with his church. As his boundaries have expanded, he has consistently made mature choices. So how does "allowing choices" enter into Ruth and James' parenting scheme with Christopher?

It is admirable that Christopher has established a pattern of making good choices. A risk that Ruth and James run is that they will fail to set *any* boundaries for Christopher, assuming that he does not need them.

Be Glad

One night a group of teenage boys gathered together to make plans for the evening.

"We could all get into Rodney's car and go to the movies."

"We could go over to Doug's house and watch a video."

"We could play Ping-Pong at Greg's."

Suggestion after suggestion was brought up for consideration. As they discussed the options someone asked, "What time do you have to be home?"

"Midnight."

"Midnight."

"Midnight."

"*Eleven!*" answered one teenager, disgustedly.

So with eleven o'clock established as the earliest curfew, they made their plans. About an hour or so later that evening, one of the boys who had *not* answered the curfew question was alone with the disgusted early bird and was evidently interested in consoling him. His words to this young man?

"Be glad your parents care enough to set a curfew for you."

True story. Kids, while they are still kids, want boundaries. Even good kids need boundaries. They need to know that their parents care enough to *want* to protect them.

Even though Christopher seems to be on track with good choices, Ruth and James will not want to withdraw all boundaries. First, because Christopher, as a teenager at home, still needs to experience their restriction and protection. And secondly, because the reinstating of boundaries after they have been abolished is very difficult.

Modeling the decision-making process and the making of good choices. Encouraging good choices. Guiding good choices. Allowing choices. Those four guidelines are essential in parenting. They are fundamental and contribute to the strong foundation most parents desire for their children. That foundation will contribute to the kids' ability to make good choices. As parents we want to construct a strong and solid foundation so that our kids can stand firm without faltering.

I once heard it said, "If you don't stand for something, you'll fall for anything." The firmer the foundation our kids are standing on, the less risk they'll "fall for anything" when it comes to making good choices. And we want them to make good choices, especially in the area of sex, drugs, and Jesus.

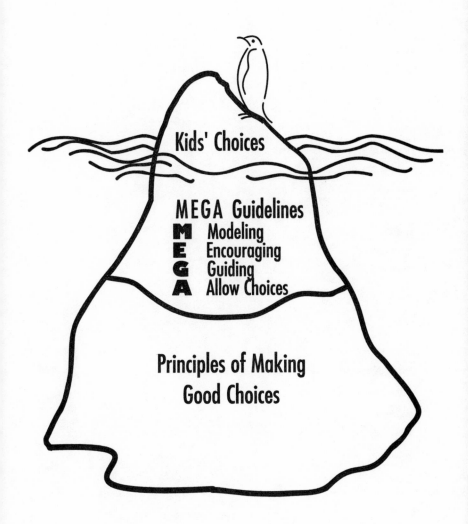

Kids' Choices

MEGA Guidelines
M Modeling
E Encouraging
G Guiding
A Allow Choices

Principles of Making
Good Choices

Kids Make Important Choices— It's Guaranteed!

Even a child is known by his actions,
by whether his conduct is pure and right.

PROVERBS 20:11

C hildren begin to make choices at an early age. Some of those choices are minor and, even at a young age, some are more significant. Typically, the choices our kids make will become more and more consequential as they mature and gain independence. Undoubtedly, our kids will make important choices—very important choices. Many of the really substantial ones "show" just like the tip of an iceberg shows above the water. Beneath the waterline lies 90 percent of the iceberg. Beneath our kids' "iceberg choices" lies the foundation we have established as parents.

Three of those tip-of-the-iceberg choices, the choices that show, are the decisions our kids will make about sex, drugs, and Jesus. These are certainly not the only important choices they will make, but for our purposes, we will use these three to illustrate the tip of the iceberg. Why? Sex, drugs, and Jesus are not typically considered gray, debatable areas. And they are most certainly key choices our kids will make. Let's take a look at how we can help our kids make good choices in these three specific areas.

TEN

Sex, Drugs, and Jesus

How can a young man keep his way pure? By living according to your word.

PSALM 119:9

The choices our kids make about sex, drugs, and Jesus are important choices at the tip of the iceberg. Our kids' choices will certainly not be limited to these three areas. They will make a multitude of choices. Most of us would agree, however, that these choices are definitely "biggies." Let's examine each one individually.

God's Word says to "abstain from fornication" (1 Thessalonians 4:3, KJV). In the New International Version the same verse instructs us to "avoid sexual immorality." That is pretty direct. When I was in graduate school, I encountered an interesting (read: convoluted) take on that particular verse.

Tina and I were both members of the same campus organization. After a couple of meetings, we identified one another as Christians and formed an acquaintance beyond our once-a-week contact. After a semester plus of friendship, Tina and I found ourselves talking one evening about a very serious topic. Tina had something on her mind and after a few minutes of chitchat, she brought it up.

"My boyfriend, Bob, has moved into my apartment," she blurted out. "What do you think about our choice?"

In reality, her confession caught me completely off guard. Quickly gathering my thoughts, I replied, "You know, Tina, it really doesn't matter what *I* think. Let's grab a Bible and see if we can find out what God thinks."

I then proceeded to get my Bible and a concordance from the shelf. I scanned the list of words and verses in the concordance until I came to "fornication." From that word I was directed to 1 Thessalonians 4:3, the verse quoted above. After we read that verse together, I reached for the dictionary to be sure we had no confusion on the words "abstain" (do without, deny oneself, forgo) or "fornication" (intercourse between two persons not married to each other). While I did this, Tina looked up the same verse in her Living Bible.

I shared the definitions with her and was very surprised by her response.

"Well, it doesn't say fornication in my Bible. It says 'sex sins,'" she said defensively. "Bob and I love each other very much, so there is no sin ... no sex sin."

What a self-serving interpretation. In spite of my friend's weak rebuttal, the verse in God's Word is very clear. God does not want us to indulge in fornication.

By the way, parents, I would strongly recommend that you use the word fornication when you are speaking about sex outside of the covenant of marriage. Do not call it "sleeping together" or "making love." Call it fornication. Why? Because that is an ugly, ugly word and better portrays the ugly, disobedient choice.

If the desire is to make good choices, godly choices, our children will abstain from fornication. That will be their choice in regard to sex. There is no gray area.

Drugs

What about drugs? Is there a Bible verse with regard to abstinence and drugs? I could not find one that was specific. God's
Word does say that our bodies are the temple of the Holy Spirit
(1 Corinthians 6:19). In 2 Corinthians 6:16 it states that "We
are the temple of the living God."

It has been proven that drugs destroy the human body. Add
to that the fact that they are an illegal substance, and we have
adequate backing to declare abstinence from drugs a good
choice.

Far too many of us know of the promising student or the ath-
lete with great potential whose future has been dangerously
detoured and perhaps even dead-ended by the use of drugs.
Remember that alcohol is also an addictive substance. And it is
the "drug of choice" of teenagers.

Kirby had been a youth leader for several years and I re-
spected his leadership abilities and his knowledge of the Word
of God. He had a genuine love and respect for teenagers and
had a vital ministry to them. As he and I discussed the problem
of drug and alcohol use and abuse among young people, he
shared with me some insight given him by one of his former
youth group kids.

"I always used to be concerned about sending my youth
group kids off to college," Kirby shared. "Just like their parents
are concerned, I guess. I knew it was a great big world out there
with temptations galore. Then one day one of my graduates
told me something that opened my eyes.

"He said that after saying 'No' to drugs and alcohol all
through *junior high* and high school [my italics], maintaining
that stand in college was easy."

There was a lot of truth there. The choices kids make about drugs are made at a very early age.

The Drug of Alcohol

On Tuesday evening Joey scored seventeen points in the eighth-grade basketball game. He was the leading scorer and with his teammates contributing another forty-six points, they were easy winners over their opponents. The boys were excited and enjoyed all the accolades at school the next day. It looked like this team was going to not only have a winning record, but compete well in the state tournament. And Joey was an integral part of the team.

But Saturday around 12:30 A.M., things didn't look quite the same. The local police noticed some kids out on the street after curfew. They didn't seem to be causing any trouble, but the policemen knew it was time for everyone under eighteen to be at home. The authorities pulled beside the kids in order to give them a stern warning and send them on their way home. When they got into close contact with the young teens, the policemen realized that they had been drinking. Now things were much more serious. They picked up the boys for underage drinking and breaking curfew and took them down to the station to call their parents.

One of the kids was Joey. The Tuesday night game would be his last one for the year. Wouldn't you think that the love of a sport and the fun of a successful performance might have dissuaded Joey from drinking? It did not. Unfortunately, the addiction to the drug of alcohol and Joey's lack of *any* foundation for making good choices won out. An eighth-grader was suspended from athletic competition for the year because of drinking. If our kids desire to make good choices, they will abstain from the use of drugs of any kind.

Choosing Jesus

And how about a choice concerning Jesus? God's Word tells us how he hopes we will all choose in this regard. "[God our Savior] ... wants all men to be saved and to come to a knowledge of the truth" (1 Timothy 2:4). What is the truth? Who is the truth? "Jesus answered, 'I am the way and the truth and the life. No one comes to the Father except through me'" (John 14:6). There is no way for us to come to God except through Jesus. "Salvation is found in no one else, for there is no other name under heaven given to men by which we must be saved" (Acts 4:12) (see appendix).

Making the choice to believe in Jesus and put our trust in him is a very good choice. It is a choice we want our children to make. It is the ultimate good choice.

A teenage boy was asked to share his testimony. He told me he didn't know if he wanted to tell his salvation story or not. I didn't understand his reticence and asked him why he wasn't more eager to share. In response he told me that he had "such a boring testimony." This young man had accepted Christ when he was four years old and had basically walked with him ever since then. No drug abuse. No alcohol addiction. No illicit sex. No rebellion from authority. How boring!

How boring? No! I explained to this young man that he had the testimony every parent wanted their child to have. As parents we want our children to make the good choice for Jesus as early as they are able. For, more times than not, that one good choice will greatly influence subsequent choices.

When we examine important choices like these about sex, drugs, and Jesus, I think it is vital that we are aware of the temptation to believe a popular lie. The lie? *Everyone* is doing it ... using it ... having it. *All* kids will have sex ... defy their parents ... use drugs ... rebel. Lies! Those all-encompassing statements are simply untrue. When we believe those lies, we are defeated before we ever begin. Know that there are plenty of kids making good choices about sex, drugs, and Jesus.

From the Start

If Lisa and Brian have been intentional in their parenting, using the MEGA guidelines, they can be certain that they have formed a solid foundation for their child. Furthermore, they can model, encourage, and guide good choices specifically in these three areas.

In order for their child to get a healthy, accurate view of sex, Lisa and Brian will want to teach him about it from the truth of God's Word. Sex was created by God. It is not bad or wrong. It is good. Sex is only bad or wrong when the rules that God has instituted are violated. Then sex is put into the destructive category. Lisa and Brian will have the opportunity to model for their child the love of a husband and wife. One of my favorite bumper stickers reads "Do your kids a favor, love your wife." We could substitute "husband" for "wife." Loving each other as husband and wife, as parents, helps to provide your child with a healthy model. Lisa and Brian's physical attraction and commitment will be in the context of marriage. If they do not condone the distortions of God's perfect model of sex through the content of modern movies, books, magazines, and other media, or in their personal behavior, their child will have a very healthy model of sex.

Lisa and Brian will have to be prepared to answer questions regarding sex that their parents did not have to answer. They will want to utilize teachable moments provided by the very world we live in to encourage their child to adopt an accurate, godly view of sex. One pitfall they will want to avoid is to provide their child with information that he has not requested and is not mature enough to process. They will not want to answer questions about sex that have not really been asked.

What's in There?

Mom and Son are traveling in the car and as they turn the corner, Son asks ...

"Mom, what is in that adult bookstore over there?"

Mom proceeds to answer that question with a barrage of information about the possible contents of that awful place.

Days later, Dad and Son are traveling in the car and as they turn that same corner Son asks ...

"Dad, what is in that adult bookstore over there?"

Dad answers, "I'm not sure. I've never been in it."

Son replies, "Then talk to Mom. She knows all about it!"

Mom provided way too much information. It was information that had not really been requested (and was not necessary).

Lisa and Brian will also be modeling, encouraging, and guiding choices in the area of drug use. It is unfortunate but true that some parents use and abuse drugs. That is a terrible model for their children. Along with abstinence from the use of illegal drugs, Lisa and Brian will want to encourage responsible use of prescription drugs—taking them only as ordered and never taking someone else's prescription. The more information they share with their child about the dangers of drug use, the more they will encourage a good choice in this area.

When we think of drugs we typically think of marijuana, cocaine, heroin, and the like. The truth of the matter is that alcohol is a drug and so is nicotine. Lisa and Brian's use or abuse of *any* drug will be a model for their child. It would serve them well to evaluate their own habits and behaviors when it comes to every available drug.

And Jesus? Lisa and Brian have both made a commitment to Christ. They have chosen him and their modeling will definitely have a positive influence on their child if they live out their faith in their daily lives. Also they can encourage the good choice of Christ by encouraging their child's involvement in activities such as worship, Sunday school, and youth group. Perhaps they will even have the opportunity to pray with their child and guide his decision for Christ.

We've talked about modeling, encouraging, and guiding choices when it comes to sex, drugs, and Jesus. Does allowing choices also apply? The choice that Lisa and Brian's child makes in regard to these three areas will definitely be his individual choice. Because the "fences" of childhood eventually expand to such an extent that direct parental influences are virtually removed, no parent can control forever their child's choices about sex, drugs, and Jesus. By modeling, encouraging, and guiding it is hoped that Lisa and Brian's child, when allowed to, will choose to say no to sex, no to drugs, and yes to Jesus. Lisa and Brian's responsibility will be to build a strong foundation for these "tip of the iceberg" choices.

Where Do You Stand?

Joan and Andy will also be able to model, encourage, and guide good choices in the areas of sex, drugs, and Jesus. It is important for their children, Neal and Allen, to know precisely where their parents stand in these three areas. Joan and Andy will not want to assume that their boys know that it is important to abstain from sex until marriage, say no to drugs, and accept Christ as their Savior.

The importance of that last choice cannot be overemphasized. Making a commitment to Christ is many times the most important step in staying out of a sexual relationship, staying drug free, or overcoming a drug dependence. Truthfully, just saying no to drugs and alcohol is not very effective unless a person has said yes to the Someone who can help him carry out the commitment. Saying yes to Christ can help an individual with his choice to say no to drugs. That is the premise of the very successful "One Way to Play—Drug Free" program of the Fellowship of Christian Athletes. Joan and Andy have modeled the choice to become Christians. They would also do well to encourage Neal and Allen to say yes to Jesus too.

Many years ago I heard a very successful church camp director speak about his program. At one point he asked me if I would like to know, in his opinion, why so many kids came to know Christ at camp. Eager to learn the secret to the spiritual success of this camping program, I quickly answered yes.

"Do you want to know why so many kids accept Christ at camp?" he asked again. "Because we ask them, 'Do you want to accept Christ?'"

Ah, the simplicity of his answer. In other words, the leaders at camp simply provided the opportunity and the kids responded.

Joan and Andy will want to look for opportunities to allow their boys to say yes to Jesus. It has been my experience that there are as many unique and individual stories of salvation, as there are individuals. Joan and Andy should not expect their sons to come to a saving knowledge of Christ in exactly the same way they did. I know of a child who accepted Christ in response to his misbehavior, knowing that even though he had made a poor choice, Jesus loved him. (His response was prompted by emotion.) One child repented and received Christ at the invitation of his Sunday school teacher. (His response was prompted by opportunity.) Then there was the child who accepted Christ because the reality of hell seemed a good thing to avoid. (An intellectual response.) Or the young man who told my husband and me that his conversion was prompted by reading sermons written by John Wesley. (A *very* intellectual response.) *What* prompts someone to accept Christ is not important. *That* he accepts Christ is very important. Joan and Andy can pray for their boys to choose to accept Christ. They cannot mandate it or force it. They can model, encourage, guide, and ultimately allow it.

Start With One Good Choice

Ruth and James have already witnessed Marci's good choice to accept Christ. This can guide all the rest of her choices including those about sex and drugs. Is it a forgone conclusion that her Christianity *will* guide all of her other choices? No. Remember my college friend Tina? She was a Christian and failed to make a good choice about sex.

The story of Tina did not end that evening with our little

chat. Tina's poor choice haunted her and made her miserable until about four months after our talk when she asked her boyfriend, Bob, to move out. That God-directed guilt, the result of her intentional disobedience, finally caused her to change her decision. Could she regain her virginity? Of course not, but God not only sees our actions but he knows our hearts. When we repent, God forgives.

> Do you not know that the wicked will not inherit the kingdom of God? Do not be deceived: Neither the sexually immoral nor idolaters nor adulterers nor male prostitutes nor homosexual offenders nor thieves nor the greedy nor drunkards nor slanderers nor swindlers will inherit the kingdom of God. And that is what some of you were. But you were washed, you were sanctified, you were justified in the name of the Lord Jesus Christ and by the Spirit of our God.
>
> 1 CORINTHIANS 6:9-11

What a wonderful verse of repentance and restoration. Did Tina initially make a good choice? No. Did she ultimately make a good choice? Yes. She had the scars to show for her poor choice, for God does not typically remove the responsibility or the repercussions of a poor choice. But he does forgive and forget our sins.

Marci will make her own choices about sex and drugs. Her love of Christ, it is hoped, will guide those choices.

Ruth and James would also do well to examine their union as husband and wife and to strengthen that commitment. That, too, can make a difference for Marci and Christopher.

In addition, where Christopher is concerned, Ruth and James may want to make the effort to connect more to his life.

They have been rather laissez-faire in their parenting and in their involvement in his life in general. In order to positively influence his choices about sex, drugs, and Jesus, Ruth and James need to be sure Christopher feels they are genuinely interested in him and are a part of his life.

A recent federally funded study of teenagers (costing more than $25 million) concluded that "teens who have a strong sense of connection to their parents are less likely to be violent or indulge in drugs, alcohol, tobacco, or early sex." This, the study found, is true all the way through high school. We can make a difference.[12]

The foundation which is laid by Lisa and Brian, Joan and Andy, and Ruth and James will influence the "tips of the iceberg" choices their kids make. All these parents can help their kids make good choices as they model, encourage, guide, and allow those good choices.

Can we guarantee our kids will make good choices especially in the areas of sex, drugs, and Jesus if we employ the MEGA guidelines? No, we are simply maximizing the possibilities. Our *only* guarantees in life are the ones we read in God's Word.

"Hey! What do ya know for *sure*?"

"Jesus loves me, this I know, for the Bible tells me so."

That is a guarantee!

The Next Right Choice—
It's a Parent's Prayer!

The effective, fervent prayer of a righteous man avails
much.

JAMES 5:16b, NKJV

When my boys were all at home, especially when they were
young, I had a pretty good idea about their needs. We
would pray together about an upcoming test or specific need
they had (for instance, to find their English notebook, to lose
their bad cough, or to help them to be kinder to an irritating
friend). As they matured, I knew less and less about their needs
and desires. How do you pray for your child when you are
unaware of all the specifics in his life? You can simply ask God
to help him do the next right thing, whatever that may be. You
see, if your child or mine will do the next right thing and follow
that with the *next* right thing and then do the NEXT right thing,
they will definitely be on the right track.

There are other prayers we can extend for our children.
There have been specific times when I have prayed for my
children to be clothed in the full armor of God. In Ephesians
6:13-17 we read about that armor.

Therefore put on the full armor of God, so that when the day
of evil comes, you may be able to stand your ground, and
after you have done everything, to stand. Stand firm then,

with the belt of truth buckled around your waist, with the breastplate of righteousness in place, and with your feet fitted with the readiness that comes from the gospel of peace. In addition to all this, take up the shield of faith, with which you can extinguish all the flaming arrows of the evil one. Take the helmet of salvation and the sword of the Spirit, which is the word of God.

In my prayer, I have mentally buckled on every piece of protective covering and handed them their sword and shield. In that armor, they are safeguarded from head to toe and they even carry an offensive weapon, the "sword of the Spirit, which is the word of God."

God's Word tells us that Satan "prowls around like a roaring lion looking for someone to devour" (1 Peter 5:8b). He comes to "steal and kill and destroy" (John 10:10a). And this evil, destructive intent is not limited to attacks on adults. The armor of God is a protection for young and old alike.

Resist the Devil

One of my favorite verses about spiritual warfare is James 4:7b. "Resist the devil, and he will flee from you." It doesn't say trample the devil or chase after the devil or beat up the devil. It simply says to resist him. Satan will actually run away from us if we merely resist him. What a 'fraidy cat! That is because he is defeated by the One living in us as believers, Jesus Christ.

That leads me to another prayer we can utter for our children, the prayer that they will come to know Christ as their Savior. This is of eternal importance. As someone once said,

"God doesn't have any grandchildren." We are either his children or not. Your faith will not save your children, but the model you have set forth, combined with your prayers, can have a very powerful, positive influence.

How long will you have to pray for your child's salvation? Will one week of diligent prayer be sufficient? How about one month or one year? No one has the answer to that question. But I do know that it is *always* too soon to give up on that prayer.

The Privilege of Praying

Praying for your child is an awesome privilege. Have you ever considered praying for your child's future spouse? Depending on the age of your child, it could be a person they have yet to meet, or even someone who will be born in the future.

Years ago Wayne Watson recorded a wonderful song with just such a message in it. The message was to pray for the child growing up "somewhere out there"—the child your child will someday marry. More than once I have reminded my youth-group kids to treat their Saturday night date with the kind of respect they hope their future spouse is being treated. Parents, we can pray for this.

Prayer for your child can include prayer for every aspect of his life. In fact, there is absolutely nothing that we cannot discuss with God. He is interested in every condition of your life and the life of your child. He, as our heavenly parent, is even more interested than we are in helping his kids make good choices.

To pray for our children to draw closer and closer to God is to bless them with the potential for a deeper relationship with the One who loves them best. God is the ultimate good choice and his Spirit can guide his children "into all truth" (John 16:13)—into all good choices.

A Praying Parent

Prayer. The importance of being a praying parent has filled entire books. In this one, however, only a tiny bit of space has been devoted to that powerful principle of parenting. The lack of emphasis does not, by any means, minimize the power or importance of prayer. Lisa and Brian can even pray for their unborn child. When it comes to making good choices, a parent's prayer is invaluable. God's Word says, "For where two or three come together in my name, there am I with them" (Matthew 18:20). And in Matthew 18:19, "If two of you on earth agree about anything you ask for, it will be done for you by my Father in heaven." That is precisely what a mother and father can do, agree together in prayer for their kids. Our children are never too young or too old to be in our prayers.

The Long Haul

A young woman, married about three years, asked me if there was a way to *know* that it was the right time to start a family. I recall that my response was a little vague except in one area.

"The right time to start a family probably varies with each couple. There are so many factors," I said. "One thing is for certain, though. Once you start, you are in it for the duration. There are no trial periods or test runs. Parenting is an all-out commitment of time, energy, and love."

There are exceptional women, there are exceptional men who have other tasks to perform in addition to the task of motherhood and fatherhood, the task of providing for the home and of keeping it. But it is the tasks connected with the home that are the fundamental tasks of humanity ... if the mother does not do her duty, there will either be no next generation or a next generation that is worse than none at all. [13]

With all that responsibility assigned to us as parents, it is important that we keep in mind those things that will aid us in our success ... choosing to Model the decision-making process and the making of good choices ... choosing to Encourage good choices ... choosing to Guide good choices ... and choosing to Allow choices.

As we love God and commit our lives to him, he will provide the model, encouragement, and guidance for our parenting task. And he will allow us to choose or reject not only himself as Savior, but his Word as the ultimate truth.

Do What You Can Do

Parents, no one will do the job of parenting perfectly. That is not our assignment. Instead, we are called to do precisely what was done by the woman in Bethany.

While he was in Bethany, reclining at the table in the home of a man known as Simon the Leper, a woman came with an alabaster jar of very expensive perfume, made of pure nard. She broke the jar and poured the perfume on his head.

Some of those present were saying indignantly to one another, "Why this waste of perfume? It could have been sold for more than a year's wages and the money given to the poor." And they rebuked her harshly.

"Leave her alone," said Jesus. "Why are you bothering her? She has done a beautiful thing to me. The poor you will always have with you, and you can help them any time you want. But you will not always have me. *She has done what she could.*"

MARK 14: 3-8a, my emphasis

We are to do what *we* can. We cannot parent perfectly, but each one of us can get better. Each one of us can personally choose to make the next right choice and then the *next* right choice, and then the NEXT right choice after that. And we can pray that our children will do the same.

"Lord, help my children make the next right choice and the *next* right choice and the NEXT one after that. Amen."

Lisa and Brian are referred to as "Christians." Joan and Andy "accepted Christ" as adults and have a "personal relationship with Jesus." Ruth "went forward" as a child at church camp. Marci "gave her heart to Jesus."

When I was a young girl, a teenager, and even a young woman, the words and phrases used above (Christians, accepted Christ, went forward, gave her heart to Jesus) meant very little to me. When I was dating my husband, I distinctly remember having a conversation with the woman who would become my mother-in-law a year or so in the future. She said something to the effect that it didn't matter what denomination you were (and then I recall she listed a few). What was important, she declared, was that you were saved.

Because I am not stupid, and because I was already completely infatuated with my boyfriend (her son), I nodded my head in complete compliance and agreement, vaguely wondering what in the world she was talking about. What she was saying was 100 percent correct. Denomination is not the issue in salvation. She had no idea, however, that I didn't understand the words she used.

Years later, shortly after we were married, I personally accepted Christ as my Savior. (See the story in *Give Your Heart a Good Spring Cleaning.*) At that point, not only did I understand the jargon, but I understood the concept and I chose to become a Christian.

Probably because of my early experience of having difficulty understanding "Christianese," I want to be sure that my language is not confusing to you. The possibility exists that you purchased this book at a bookstore or at a conference because of the straightforward title, or the pretty cover. Or maybe your kids had just pushed you over the edge or disappointed you one more time with their bad choices.

You may have had no idea that this book would look at parenting and good choices from a Christian perspective. That's OK. I just don't want to put down my pen until I take the opportunity to explain to you what Lisa and Brian, Joan and Andy, Ruth, Marci, and I chose to do:[14]

Step 1
God's Purpose: Peace and Eternal Life

God loves you, and he wants you to live in peace with him and to receive eternal life.

The Bible says ...

We have peace with God through our Lord Jesus Christ.
ROMANS 5:1b

For God so loved the world that he gave his only begotten Son, that whoever believes in him should not perish but have everlasting life.
JOHN 3:16

The gift of God is eternal life in Christ Jesus our Lord.
ROMANS 6:23b

God planned for us to be at peace with him and to have eternal life.

Step 2
Our Problem: Sin and Separation

God did not make us robots to mindlessly love and obey him. Instead he gave us a will and freedom of choice. But we often choose to disobey God and go our own selfish ways. This side of our nature is called sin, and it separates us from God.

The Bible says ...

For all have sinned and fall short of the glory of God [and] the wages of sin is death.

ROMANS 3:23; 6:23

But your iniquities have separated you from your God; your sins have hidden his face from you, so that he will not hear.

ISAIAH 59:2

Our sin separates us from God.

Step 3
God's Remedy: The Cross

Jesus Christ is the only answer to this problem of separation from God. He died on the cross and rose from the grave to pay the penalty for our sin—completely bridging the gap between us and God.

The Bible says ...

But God demonstrates his own love for us in this: While we were still sinners, Christ died for us.

ROMANS 5:8

Salvation is found in no one else, for there is no other name under heaven given to men by which we must be saved.

ACTS 4:12

God is on one side and all the people on the other side, and Christ Jesus, Himself man, is between them to bring them together.

1 TIMOTHY 2:5, TLB

I [Jesus] tell you the truth, whoever hears my word and believes him who sent me has eternal life and will not be condemned; he has crossed over from death to life.

JOHN 5:24

God has provided the only way.... And we must make the choice.

Step 4
Our Response: Receive Jesus Christ

When we believe in Jesus' message and trust in him alone to save us, we can receive him.

The Bible says ...

All the prophets testify about him that everyone who believes in him [Jesus Christ] receives forgiveness of sins through his name.

ACTS 10:43

[Jesus said] Do not let your hearts be troubled. Trust in God; trust also in me.

JOHN 14:1

But as many as received him, to them he gave the right to become children of God, to those who believe in his name.

JOHN 1:12, NKJV

How to receive Christ:

1. Admit your need. (I am a sinner.)
2. Be willing to turn from your sins. (Repent.)
3. Believe that Jesus Christ died for you on the cross and rose from the grave.
4. Through prayer, invite Jesus Christ to come in and control your life through the Holy Spirit. (Receive him as your Savior.)

So if you desire to have eternal life and the help of God's Holy Spirit in *this* life, you can pray a simple prayer.

What to Pray:

Dear Lord Jesus, I know that I am sinful and I need your forgiveness. I believe that you died to pay the penalty for my sin. I want to turn from my sin nature and follow you instead. I invite you to come into my heart and life. In Jesus' name. Amen.

That's it!

God's Assurance: His Word

If you sincerely prayed this prayer and asked Jesus Christ to come into your life, do you know what he has given you?

The Bible says ...
Everyone who calls on the name of the Lord will be saved.

ROMANS 10:13

Neither height nor depth, nor anything else in all creation, will be able to separate us from the love of God that is in Christ Jesus our Lord.

ROMANS 8:39

Therefore, since we have been justified through faith, we have peace with God through our Lord Jesus Christ.

ROMANS 5:1

He who has the Son has life; he who does not have the Son of God does not have life. These things I have written to you who believe in the name of the Son of God, that you may know that you have eternal life.

1 JOHN 5:12-13, NKJV

Welcome to the family. See you in heaven, if not before.

Kendra

Notes

1. Gayle G. Roper, *Balancing Your Emotions* (Wheaton, Ill.: Harold Shaw Publishers, 1992), 44.
2. Kendra Smiley, *Give Your Heart a Good Spring Cleaning* (Ann Arbor, Mich.: Servant Books, 1999), 81.
3. Dr. Laura Schlessinger, *USA Weekend*, January 15–17, 1999, 5.
4. James Dobson and Gary L. Bauer, *Children at Risk* (Nashville, Tenn.: Word, 1990), 159.
5. Wayne Rice and David Veerman, *Understanding Your Teenager* (Nashville, Tenn.: Word, 1999), 90.
6. Bob Smithouser, "The Last Word," *Plugged In*, September 1999, 12.
7. Kendra Smiley, *It's a Mom Thing!* (Colorado Springs, Colo.: Cook Communications, 2000), 53.
8. Paul Meier, *Don't Let Jerks Get the Best of You*, (Nashville, Tenn.: Thomas Nelson, 1993), 22.
9. Bob Smithouser, "Wise Parents Continue to 'Check Out the Ride,'" *Plugged In*, Focus on the Family, December 15, 1998, 12.
10. Meier, 144.
11. Rice and Veerman, 58.
12. Rice and Veerman, 206.
13. Theodore Roosevelt, as quoted in Dobson and Bauer, 155.
14. Adapted from Billy Graham's *Steps to Peace*, as received over the internet.

About the Author

Live Life Intentionally! That describes the message the author and national speaker Kendra Smiley brings to her audiences. According to Kendra, "Life is a wonderful smorgasbord of choices and everyone is responsible *for* and empowered *by* the choices they make."

Kendra challenges and encourages people to make the next right choice out of the myriad of choices in life. She has a unique, humorous approach that appeals to readers and listeners of all ages. Her messages teach Bible-based skills essential to successful living and they provide the motivation to make positive life changes.

Kendra has a B.S. from the University of Illinois and an M.S. from the University of North Dakota. She and her husband, John, have been married for twenty-seven years. They have three sons, Matthew, Aaron, and Jonathan. The Smiley family lives on a farm in central Illinois.

For more information about having Kendra speak to your group, visit Kendra's website at www.KendraSmiley.com or contact her at:

Kendra Smiley
P.O. Box 104
East Lynn, IL 60932
toll free 1-877-GRAB JOY
(472-2569)